2014

D0221256

REDUCING EMPLOYEE THEFT

REDUCING

EMPLOYEE THEFT
A Guide to Financial and Organizational Controls

Neil H. Snyder,
O. Whitfield Broome, Jr.,
William J. Kehoe,
James T. McIntyre, Jr.,
AND Karen E. Blair

Foreword by Harry E. Figgie, Jr.

QUORUM BOOKS
NEW YORK • WESTPORT, CONNECTICUT • LONDON

Library of Congress Cataloging-in-Publication Data

Reducing employee theft : a guide to financial and organizational
   controls / Neil H. Snyder . . . [et al.].
      p.   cm.
   Includes index.
   ISBN 0–89930–588–1 (alk. paper)
   1. Employee theft—United States.   I. Snyder, Neil H.
HF5549.5.E43R44   1991
658.4′73—dc20   90–26208

British Library Cataloguing in Publication Data is available.

Copyright © 1991 by Neil H. Snyder, O. Whitfield Broome, Jr., William J. Kehoe,
James T. McIntyre, Jr., and Karen E. Blair

All rights reserved. No portion of this book may be
reproduced, by any process or technique, without the
express written consent of the publisher.

Library of Congress Catalog Card Number: 90–26208
ISBN: 0–89930–588–1

First published in 1991

Quorum Books, One Madison Avenue, New York, NY 10010
An imprint of Greenwood Publishing Group, Inc.

Printed in the United States of America

The paper used in this book complies with the
Permanent Paper Standard issued by the National
Information Standards Organization (Z39.48–1984).

10 9 8 7 6 5 4 3 2 1

Contents

Foreword

Employee theft is a luxury American business finds increasingly difficult to afford.

Not simply because it costs companies more than $40 billion annually; not simply because almost one in three business failures may be directly linked to internal stealing, according to a U.S. Chamber of Commerce study, but because the problem of employee theft goes to the heart of American business competitiveness and our ability to compete in a global economy.

I first became aware of Neil Snyder and his important work on employee theft several years ago when I was an Executive-in-Residence at the McIntire School of Commerce at the University of Virginia. I was impressed with his insights and approach to a business problem which is too often viewed as insignificant or beyond anyone's control. It is neither.

Theft is a core issue for the success of the American free enterprise system. As Professor Snyder and his colleagues demonstrate, "employee theft" refers to more than criminally minded employees or a faulty hiring process. The problem of theft also represents a pervasive failure to properly manage businesses and motivate employees. Beyond that, it is a disturbing product of society's failure to adequately educate its citizens in efficient, productive work habits.

Reducing Employee Theft places the problem in its larger organizational perspective, analyzing it as a strategic and operational issue, not simply one of keeping thieves off the payroll.

We all know of the petty and seemingly irrelevant acts of filching paper clips, an occasional bit of postage, personal toll calls or an item of inventory. We are all familiar with the too liberally invoked expense-account lunch and have read the headlines about the embezzlement of company or government funds by an apparently upstanding employee.

Aside from these familiar kinds of theft, the authors discuss other, less visible, forms of thievery. Employees steal a firm's time through inefficient use of the workday and by the outright avoidance of work. Even loyal managers and supervisors can rob a company. They sap the firm of valuable resources when they treat employees in such a way that the latter are not motivated to either produce or protect the firm, its assets or its potential.

On the most concrete level, *Reducing Employee Theft* is a practical guide to the strategies and resources available to deter those tempted to steal and to apprehend those who succumb to temptation.

It makes an important contribution as a treatise designed to help businesses engineer their working environments to instill solid values and forge employee commitment to the goals of the enterprise. The most effective inoculations against the disease of employee theft are not elaborate security systems and complex cross-checks on work assignments, but are the inculcation and reinforcement of the attitudes and work habits that breed commitment to the goals of the business.

In several respects, this volume complements a series of investigations commissioned by our company—Figgie International—during the 1980s. For many years, Figgie International has been deeply concerned about crime in American society. Throughout the 1980s we sponsored a series of studies on crime in America, investigating its effects on citizens, business and communities. This scourge poses a tremendous threat to our quality of life.

Reducing Employee Theft expands the perspective of these studies to the next logical arena, the workplace. Although seemingly invisible and devoid of physical violence, employee theft is nonetheless a virulent and destructive menace. It is estimated that over one-third of employees steal from their employers. In one study of the retail industry, the average value of what a shoplifter took was about $57—but the value of what a dishonest employee took was more than $890!

Like the Figgie Reports, *Reducing Employee Theft* throws a spotlight on a very pervasive and debilitating social problem in our increasingly materialistic society.

In viewing theft reduction as an integral strategic and operational tool for business, *Reducing Employee Theft* is a new and important resource in the daily battle of American business competing in a global economy.

Harry E. Figgie, Jr.
Chairman of the Board and
Chief Executive Officer
Figgie International Inc.

Preface

Employee theft is an often overlooked, but serious, problem facing businesses in the United States today. Reliable estimates suggest that about one-third of all business failures can be attributed directly to employee theft and that employees steal more than $40 billion annually from their employers—that is ten times the cost of street crime in America. In addition, the problem is escalating at a 15 percent annual rate.

To understand the effects of theft on the financial condition of a business, it should be viewed as dollars subtracted directly from the bottom line. In most cases, however, it is hidden in the line item on the income statement for cost of goods sold and passed on to consumers in the form of higher prices. As long as a firm's competitors do not control theft either, then they are not at a price disadvantage because everyone's prices will be too high. But if the competitors take theft seriously and deal with it, then they have a price advantage and will attract more customers as a result. For this reason, many firms are fortunate employee theft gets so little attention.

Additionally, many opportunities are forfeited because of employee theft. Every dollar lost to theft is a dollar that could have been used to expand the business, buy the latest piece of equipment that could have made the business more competitive, improve employee training, and so on. Firms that have a serious theft problem will find that solving it can provide as much money for investment purposes as most firms can borrow from a bank—and there are no interest charges on funds obtained from reduced theft.

Looked at another way, employee theft robs businesses of the marginal dollars generated by increased sales. Consider, for example, employee theft in a heavily regulated business like banking. Despite all the assistance provided by bank examiners and the advice of top accounting firms, an employee of Manufacturers Hanover Corporation recently stole about $50 million. Assuming a 2 percent spread, the bank will have to generate about $2.5 billion in new business just to cover the loss. Imagine what a loss of this magnitude would have done to a less solvent bank. It's no wonder that so many business failures are attributed to employee theft.

Unfortunately, most owners and managers avoid dealing with employee theft because it is an unpleasant task and because they think that they can safely ignore it. During good times, it is possible to ignore the problem without imposing undue and unnecessary risks on the business because margins are high enough to support theft. When times are bad, however, many firms struggle to survive, and employee theft can literally become the straw that breaks the back of a business.

Another reason owners and managers prefer not to deal with employee theft is that there is no simple definition of theft. Business owners possess a wide range of values and beliefs, and so do their employees. They all see the world differently, and they define theft differently. Therefore, actions that are viewed as theft in one business may not be viewed as theft in another. But most business owners naively assume that their employees see things the way they do, and this assumption leads to much larceny.

To make matters worse, otherwise honest people will steal from their employers and believe sincerely that they are doing nothing wrong. For example, when employees believe that they are not being rewarded properly for their work, some of them will "steal." But, in their opinions, they are not stealing; they are merely getting what they deserve. Other employees might retaliate against their employers when they are angry by "stealing." But, in their minds, they are not stealing either; they are only getting even. Each of these examples represents theft by employees, but they are not examples of theft by people who are bona fide thieves.

No matter why it happens, theft affects attitudes and morale in businesses negatively. When a business has theft problems, most of its employees know about it, and the honest ones do not like it. They would prefer not to work with thieves, and they resent the fact that owners and managers are not dealing with the problem. When this happens, honest employees will either assume that the owners and managers of the business know about the problem and do not care, or that they do not know about it and are incompetent. Many of them will just quit, but others (the less honest ones) will do as their fellow employees are doing—steal.

Dealing with employee theft is essential. Failing to deal with it can literally destroy a business. Reducing theft requires a careful review of the entire range of strategies, structures, and management practices used by the firm to determine whether they encourage or discourage theft.

Contrary to popular opinion, dealing with employee theft does not mean catching thieves, although thieves will be found in any business and their employment should be terminated. The most effective way to deal with employee theft is to create an organization that will not support thieves and to choke them out of the business. In other words, owners and managers should make working for their business so unattractive to thieves that they will not want to stay.

We hope you will use this book as a guide to identify employee theft problems in your organization and to implement various strategies and procedures to reduce it. If you use the ideas in this book, you could save your business or considerably increase your profitability.

Acknowledgments

Writing a book is a long and arduous task that requires the dedication and commitment of a whole host of people. We want to thank our colleagues at the McIntire School of Commerce of the University of Virginia for their encouragement and support. We also want to thank Cam Garrard and Barbara Gilbert for their hard work and assistance during manuscript preparation. We owe a special debt of gratitude to Dean William G. Shenkir of the McIntire School of Commerce for his support and encouragement, but most of all for his generous support of student research assistants who worked with us as we developed this project.

The thoughts that go into a book do not come to the authors all at once. Typically, the concept of a book is developed over many years, and the ideas that establish the character and content of a book often appear in many forms before they culminate in a final product that is "the book." This project has been no exception. A version of the material in chapter 1 appeared in the May-June 1989 issue of *Business Horizons* under the title "Dealing with Employee Theft" by Neil H. Snyder and Karen E. Blair. Jim Dowd, a colleague of ours at the McIntire School, is responsible for developing the case material that appears in chapter 2. The experience of Roger Self and Donna Bietel contributed an important dimension to chapter 3. Caroline Bohi, Katherine Davisson, and Mary Farsetta worked closely with Neil H. Snyder in the development of the material in chapter 4. The ethics materials in chapter 5 were developed by William J. Kehoe as the result of research grants from the McIntire School of Commerce and from the Center for Advanced Studies of the University of Virginia. Margaret Bumgardner DuBose of McNair Law

Firm in Columbia, South Carolina, worked closely with Jim McIntyre in the development of the material in chapter 6. A version of the material in chapter 7 appeared in the July 1989 issue of *Journal of Small Business Management* under the title "Using Internal Controls to Reduce Employee Theft in Small Businesses" by Neil H. Snyder, O. Whitfield Broome, Jr., and Karen E. Zimmerman. A version of the material in chapter 8 appeared in the August 1989 issue of *Industrial Management* under the title "Using Physical Security Devices to Reduce Employee Theft" by Neil H. Snyder and Janet Caswell. And finally, a version of the material in chapter 9 appeared in the October-November-December 1990 issue of *Business* under the title "It May Look Like Time Theft, but It Probably Isn't" by Neil H. Snyder, Karen E. Blair, and Tina Arndt.

CHAPTER 1

Dealing with Employee Theft

The most serious threat to the business community . . . does not come from outside sources, but instead comes from within the organization itself.[1]

THE PROBLEM

CASE EXAMPLE 1

In 1973 a hardworking, ambitious employee of a small paint business purchased the company, keeping many of the workers. In 1977 he discovered a large inventory embezzlement; $60,000 to $70,000 had been stolen. An investigation revealed that 72 percent of his employees were stealing from the company. The bulk of them had been with the company for many years.

CASE EXAMPLE 2

In 1983 a mail-order company suffered substantial losses because of internal theft. The market was new, and the company had few competitors. Because the organization was obliged to expand rapidly to keep pace with demand, difficulties arose. The owner said, "We ran into problems because communication within the organization had deteriorated. The company was growing too fast. We were delegating too many things, and the company got out of balance. We had to have massive employee turnover and had to put our philosophical priorities straight."

Both of these scenarios are typical. The first involves an established company acquired by a new owner. The new business is subject to all of the problems caused by the previous owner, including lax management, poor inventory and financial controls, and an absence of clearly defined values and beliefs within the company.

The second involves a company started from scratch. Its management system and code of ethics were established by the owner. Because the organization was growing so rapidly, however, the internal structure became difficult to maintain, and "the company got out of balance."

Employee theft is a rampant problem throughout American businesses, large and small. According to the U.S. Chamber of Commerce, an estimated $40 billion is stolen annually from U.S. businesses, ten times the cost of the nation's street crime.[2] Rod Willis, managing editor for *Management Review*, says that, though the range varies, some loss estimates exceed $200 billion.[3] Even more frightening is the fact that these internal losses are increasing at a 15 percent annual rate.[4]

Gregory Arnold, an instructor in the Police Science Department at Lake City Community College in Florida, cites law enforcement officials who maintain that "more than ninety percent of today's crime occurs inside businesses rather than on the street." He goes on to say, "These internal thefts range from minor pilferage of office supplies by clerical personnel to major fraud by persons in upper management."[5]

William Beane, corporate security director at United Airlines, emphasizes that "although larger amounts of stolen goods tend to draw greater attention and publicity to the employee theft problem, the cumulative effect of the smaller inside jobs can be more devastating."[6]

Another study by the U.S. Chamber of Commerce suggested that "up to 75% of all employees steal at least once, and half of these steal at least twice."[7] As one observer noted, "in short, it is no longer a question of 'it only happens to someone else,' because the odds are that someone else will be you."[8]

Another issue that attracts attention is time theft. Although recognized by practicing managers as a significant problem, there is a great deal of controversy about what constitutes time theft and how to deal with it in a manner that improves individual performance. In a 1985 survey, Robert Half of Robert Half International estimated that "U.S. employees stole $170 billion worth of their employers' time last year."[9] A staggering sum. The *ABA Banking Journal* provides a list of some of the more common ways employees steal time from their employers.[10] Employees might be:

1. Socializers
2. Coffee drinkers

3. Telephone talkers

4. Readers

5. Restroom-minded

6. Water drinkers

7. Dreamers

8. Fastidious (taking thirty minutes to type one letter)

9. Anticipators (packing to leave twenty minutes before time to go)

10. Long lunchers

11. Holidayers

12. Nonsick

13. Visitors

Of course, an employee is not necessarily stealing time whenever he or she makes a personal phone call or goes to the water cooler for a drink. If a business owner had this belief and acted on it, the morale of his or her employees would be low, and they might feel like they were going to prison each morning instead of to work. Under these conditions, productivity would decline and profitability would suffer. Clearly, dealing with time theft requires careful thought, good judgment, and an understanding of the motives of one's employees. For example, although it is perfectly legitimate for them to call a doctor to make an appointment, it would be inappropriate for them to call a friend and carry on a lengthy conversation that has nothing to do with business.

Despite the legitimate exceptions, most business owners and managers will recognize some of their employees on this list. In addition, many of them will share the attitude of a small business owner who says, "There's not much I can do about time theft." Or they may believe, as does an investigator for a police department in Virginia, that time theft is "just a cost of doing business."

This attitude is inappropriate because it inevitably results in passive acceptance of a potentially critical problem. In fact, acceptance of this behavior from marginal employees will cause the most productive employees to lose respect for the owner or manager and to develop similar behavior patterns. Time theft can be reduced if management takes an active stand against it. Robert Half agrees. He says that "a manager who recognizes that time theft is wrong, that it is literally theft, and that it can be met head-on is halfway home to improving productivity."[11]

The same is true for more tangible losses. The *American Journal of Small Business* says that "if a company anticipates, and in essence plans for, a certain loss figure, it will probably experience that level of loss. It is logical that steps should be taken to prevent or control losses instead of simply allowing them to rise to their level of expectation."[12] The bottom line is that passive acceptance of theft at any level is counterproductive.

Any form of internal theft, tangible or intangible, can devastate small businesses and can cause bankruptcy or failure. Insurance companies estimate that almost one-third of all business failures in the United States are due to internal theft.[13] In an interview on March 31, 1988, Bill Barker, member affairs director for the Retail Merchants Association of Greater Richmond, Virginia, painted an even bleaker picture. He said, "over half of small businesses that go out of business fail because of internal theft. Shoplifting will steal your profits; employees will steal your business." As the police investigator cited earlier says, "if you could do away with employee theft, businesses would flourish."

Most experts agree, however, that the reduction of theft is a much more realistic goal than eliminating it altogether.[14] But, to reduce internal theft, business owners and their management staffs must recognize that the problem exists and must take an active role in prevention and control.

First, they must understand who might steal from them and how they might do it. Second, they must implement control procedures that are appropriate for their particular employees. According to Charles A. Sennewald, "there is a relationship between theft and trust. The one you trust the least will steal the least and the one you trust the most could end up stealing the most."[15] This may be an extreme perspective, but he makes a valid point. The people who are in the best position to steal large sums of money from the business and who could steal the most before being detected are the ones trusted the most. Owners and managers would be wise to recognize that anyone (i.e., partners, officers, relatives, friends) could steal from the company. Also, business owners must believe that employee theft, in any form, is not just a "cost of doing business," but most often also a result of problems within the organization itself. Therefore, business owners and managers must adapt their management strategies to create an environment that will reduce and prevent employee theft.

HIRING THE RIGHT PEOPLE

For any theft reduction program to work, management must have good people to work with. Therefore, potential thieves should be identified before they are hired. In general, such prescreening measures as personal interviews, reference checks, credit checks, and pencil-and-paper honesty tests can effectively and inexpensively reduce employee theft. (See Appendix 1, "How to Hire and Keep Quality Employees," by Ryan A. Kuhn, president of Reid Psychological Systems in Chicago.)

Personal Interviews

Probably the most important prescreening device available is the personal interview. Interviews should be conducted in a professional and consistent manner, and the information obtained from them should be used in conjunction with the information gathered in other ways.

The police investigator mentioned previously shared an example of a theft at a gas station owned by a major oil and gas company that suggests the importance of using multiple prescreening devices. The station manager needed someone to fill a part-time position, and he did not want to take the time to do a thorough prescreening job. He interviewed a person off the street whom he did not know and hired him on the spot. The manager's decision to hire the man was based solely on the impression he made in a short interview. Two days later he stole more than $3,000 and disappeared. The person had given not only an incorrect phone number, but also an assumed name.

Thieves can be good dissemblers. First impressions, though often accurate, should not be the only method used to screen potential employees. The best prescreening system includes a combination of the measures mentioned in this chapter that are tailored to the individual needs of a company.

Reference Checks

Reference checks are always a good idea, but they often vary in the amount of useful information provided. Typically, business owners say that reference checks are not effective. Most organizations are so worried about being liable for invading a previous employee's privacy that they are unwilling to provide much information beyond the social security number and the dates of employment.

On the other hand, reference checks can be quite helpful. In an article for *Across the Board*, Irving Radler stresses their importance: "A good check on prospective employees is essential in weeding out the potential thief. There are criminals who go from firm to firm, always one step ahead of being caught, who create havoc with company records and finances. By the simple task of verifying their last employment and talking to their last employer, one can usually detect if something was amiss."[16]

In addition, talking with previous employers can help to identify work and nonwork-related problems like alcoholism and drug addiction. Both of these conditions affect performance in a significant way, and both have the potential to create needs within people that result in stealing. The cost of supporting a drug habit is enormous, and wise business owners and managers are beginning to realize the importance of directly addressing this potentially devastating issue.

Because of the difficulty in uncovering facts when making reference checks, employers should learn to listen to what is not being said. By simply refusing to provide information, a person's previous employers are able to reveal a great deal about them. For instance, if employment dates and other nonsensitive information is all you can obtain, then you have reason to question whether you have enough good data to make a decision to hire a person. To adapt an adage, "when in doubt, do not make an offer."

Credit Checks

Another helpful screening device is a credit check. A person who is viewed as a credit risk because of poor debt repayment practices is not necessarily a thief, but many argue that not repaying one's debts according to the terms of the agreement is a form of theft. Most business people would agree that a prospective employee who is too heavily in debt is more likely to steal than one who is not. Though they can reduce the odds of hiring a thief, credit checks cannot solve the problem. As one business executive points out: "A credit check merely tells a company that someone pays his or her bills on time; the person could be paying those bills with money taken from his or her employers."[17] Nonetheless, credit checks should be part of any hiring process. When the information is available, it can be an accurate indicator of a prospective employee's potential for theft and suitability for the position offered.

Pencil-and-Paper Honesty Tests

Pencil-and-paper honesty tests are good screening devices. One small business owner who uses them in his hiring process says that the tests "are not demeaning if done in a professional manner. And most employees accept that some sort of testing is a normal part of the process."

A typical honesty test costs from $6 to $15 per person to administer, depending on how much service the client gets. Scoring can be done by the publisher over the telephone, or the company can do the scoring.[18] Three respected honesty test publishers are (1) Reid Psychological Systems of Chicago; (2) Stanton Corporation of Charlotte, North Carolina; and (3) London House of Park Ridge, Illinois.

Earl Welliver, vice president for security at Platt Music Company in Torrance, California, says that by using the Stanton test, his company has reduced its turnover: "We have been able to save money on our training because we have a better selection process."[19]

Polygraph Tests

The polygraph test is certainly the most controversial prescreening device currently available. In June 1988 the president of the United States signed legislation that made all but about 25 percent of the 2 million polygraph tests administered annually in the United States illegal, and virtually eliminated their use for prescreening employees.

However, the controversy surrounding polygraph tests still remains. Some business owners believe that the polygraph test is essential. For example, the paint company president previously cited believes in the polygraph "100 percent" and has used the tool almost exclusively to reduce theft in his organization. He believes that it is the best solution to the problem of employee dishonesty: "I had a man who, after failing the polygraph twice, swore that he had not stolen from me. I told him that, under the circumstances, I had to terminate his employment. Two weeks later, I got a call from the police. The guy was wanted and had been working under an assumed name." Clearly, the polygraph test has been an effective tool in this particular organization, although the company president admitted that several of his trusted employees resented it.

Therein lies the danger of using polygraph tests. They can kill morale. If they were used consistently within an organization as a preventive device, they could create bad feelings among honest employees and breed suspicion and discontent.

When polygraph tests have been used to screen potential employees, employers have run the risk of making them feel as though the company assumes that they are dishonest. The honest person may never develop a genuine loyalty to the company under these conditions because he or she cannot identify with an organization that subjects its employees to such a degrading experience. James Ritchey, president of Workable Systems in Raleigh, North Carolina, describes the problem this way: "The problem with taking a polygraph test on the way in is that they're being told they're not being trusted. . . . Therefore, their philosophy is that these are bad people, the company is a bad thing and somehow it justifies stealing."[20]

Despite the passage of legislation forbidding the use of polygraph tests in most instances, they may have a place in business. If an owner or a manager has good reasons to suspect that a person has stolen from the company, then a polygraph test for that person may be appropriate. Polygraph tests cannot be used as a general screening device. They can be used, however, to confirm or refute a suspicion that a person is stealing from the company, and using them in this way is not likely to cause significant negative reactions from other employees.

Take Time to Do a Thorough Job

The thoroughness of the prescreening process is crucial in reducing employee theft. Most employers view hiring as a "necessary evil," an unpleasant process. They often are anxious to get it over with as quickly as possible. Time, more than expense, is the primary issue, and wise managers will take time to address potential problems with employees before the hiring decision is made. As another adage says, "an ounce of prevention is worth a pound of cure."

ESTABLISHING AND MANAGING THE ORGANIZATIONAL CLIMATE

Theft is a state of mind—nothing more. Prevention and control are merely states of awareness and caring.[21]

Physical security cannot solve the problem because the physical acts do not constitute the problem; the mental attitude behind them does.[22]

"American managers have let us down," says the owner of a successful mail-order firm. "They need to re-think how to govern and manage. . . . People are their most important resource. If you treat people like you would want to be treated, then you will be okay." This business owner believes that the single most important factor in controlling internal theft is management's attitude toward employees. People must be treated as a resource, not as a commodity. They must believe that the organization cares about them as people and that they will not be treated like tools to be used and discarded.

Comparing his firm with one that had a completely different attitude toward theft, he gave an example of another mail-order company. The company has so many demeaning and excessive security checks that the amount of control is perceived by the employees as excessive and absurd. "We can operate a warehouse which handles the same number of orders with eight employees as opposed to their forty-two. We can run a much more productive, efficient operation, pay higher salaries and treat our workers like people, not animals."

Establishing the right environment in your business is an important and inexpensive step in reducing internal theft. As one small business owner said, "the more money spent on a security system, the more counter-productive it is." He estimates that "almost 98 percent of the theft problems in American business today can be taken care of inexpensively if you have a tightly run, caring organization." The bottom line is that people do not tend to steal from the people they admire and respect. By taking actions that communicate clearly in tangible and intangible ways that the employees really do matter, owners and managers can make great strides in improving morale and reducing theft.

Establishing Company Values and Beliefs

The first step in creating an organizational climate conducive to high productivity and morale is to formulate a set of company values and beliefs that communicates to everyone what the firm stands for and what is expected from its employees. Thus company values and beliefs should be written and distributed to all prospective employees. In addition, owners and managers must make a conscious effort to promote them and to ensure their acceptance by rewarding employees for successfully adopting the company's values and beliefs. If honesty and integrity are important, then it should be clearly stated and understood by everyone.

Establishing an atmosphere of honesty and integrity within a business is of paramount importance in reducing theft, and it must filter down from top management to all employees without regard to their salary or their position in the hierarchy. Owners and managers should set an example for employees. They should not allow themselves to adopt a double standard, with one set of rules for employees and another set for owners and managers. If a double standard exists, an inconsistent message is communicated and increased employee theft is likely to result. Without exception, owners and managers should adhere to the same high standards they expect their employees to honor. The mail-order company owner put it this way: "Before you dictate beliefs, you have to live them."

In larger businesses the example set by an employee's immediate supervisor has a direct effect on how that employee views the company. Peter Bullard and Alan Resnik explain: "The role of the front-line supervisor is absolutely critical to company morale and effective communication in all businesses. . . . Employees form most of their opinions about the organization on the basis of their supervisor's behavior."[23] Thus it is absolutely essential for all members of the management team to adhere closely to the established values and beliefs. If they deviate even slightly from the established value system, the employees may conclude that the system is meaningless. Furthermore, if employees know that an owner or a manager is stealing from the company, they can use this information to their advantage if caught stealing themselves.

Neutralizing Rationalization

Like the tax evader or the street criminal, employee thieves have an endless set of justifications for their actions. They do not see themselves as crim-

inals . . . [but] feel that by stealing they are getting what they deserve—
and the company is getting what it deserves too.[24]

Rationalization is a big problem. In a book review for *Across the Board*,
David C. Anderson gives the example of a consultant from England who
buys an "all-over" ticket that gives unlimited travel in the United States.
Using his prepurchased ticket, he flies around the United States but
charges individual companies full price for the tickets he would have
purchased if he had only one U.S. destination. He makes a nice profit
by pocketing the difference and justifies his actions by saying, "They
don't mind paying at all—it's peanuts to them for a big order—but it
means quite a bit to me."[25] In the absence of well-defined and well-
communicated values and beliefs to the contrary, honest people can
rationalize many acts that most owners and managers would call stealing. Establishing company values and beliefs can help to neutralize the
tendency people have to rationalize.

Fostering Morale by Opening the Lines of Communication

Two-way communication within the organization is important as well.
Daniel van Buren, corporate director of loss prevention for Ira A. Watson
Company in Knoxville, Tennessee, says, "Giving employees an opportunity to discuss their problems and acknowledging they merit consideration provides positive reinforcement for employees and makes them
feel more a part of the company."[26]

One cannot overstate the importance of morale. If an employee is
happy, there is less reason to steal from the company. And, as van
Buren says, "people tend not to steal from themselves; thus, the more
they identify with the company, the better."[27]

John Kennish, director of security for Commerce Bancshares, Inc., in
Kansas City, Missouri, states that "managers should recognize and acknowledge the great majority of employees who don't steal and reinforce
this attitude. An effective two-way communication method used toward
this end involves not always telling employees what to do, but also
asking for employees' input and then using their ideas."[28]

Positive feedback works in a similar way to motivate employees and
to foster high morale among them. "Recognition of good things is vital,"
says one small business owner. "It's so damn simple. It's tragic how
few companies understand it."

In today's business world many employees feel ignored or taken for
granted. They must be rewarded, whether through sales incentives or
through individual recognition as in "employee of the month" programs.
By recognizing the contributions of employees to the success of the
business in tangible and intangible ways, management can increase mo-

rale, reduce negative feelings that affect how employees perceive their company, and reduce the likelihood that employee theft will occur.

The central issue is that loyalty to the company has the effect of reducing employee theft. As one security manager said, "there is no panacea for weeding out dishonest people. It has to be the loyalty to the company." If the firm's welfare becomes important to employees, theft should be reduced.

KEEPING HONEST EMPLOYEES HONEST

If fighting dishonest employees is an important task of management, educating the honest ones is vital.[29]

A large percentage of internal thefts are committed by honest people who often are unaware that their actions are unacceptable. Examples of this abound. From the fast-food restaurant employee who takes a hamburger home at night to the car parts store employee who takes a spark plug, there is a widely held belief that taking goods from inventory for personal use is not stealing. Roy Carter, who writes on corporate assets protection for the International Business and Professional Press, explains: "Employee theft is virtually universal, and in an environment where almost everyone behaves habitually in the same way, the activity, even if illegal, often appears legitimate."[30] In an article for *Accountancy*, Carter quotes a man who testified in juvenile court for his son, who had been caught shoplifting pencils: "There was no need for him to do it. I can get him all the pencils he wants from work."[31]

This man's attitude is typical. Employees often believe that such items are insignificant to the company, and that they should be included as benefits. Dealing with employees who possess this attitude requires sensitivity and understanding. They are honest people who do not regard these actions as stealing. Establishing and communicating the right values is the first step in reducing this kind of problem.

Focus Employee Attention on the Cost of Theft to Individuals

Most otherwise honest employees who steal from their employers do not experience guilt. They do not understand that the little extras they take can make a difference, even to a large corporation. Roy Carter says that the task of management "is to describe to them the cumulative impact of their actions, which ultimately threaten the livelihoods of all concerned."[32]

Employees need to understand the effects of losses on the company, but they also need to understand the cost to them personally. Managers should focus attention on profit sharing and other bonuses per employee that would have been available had the losses been prevented. These are "easily understandable proofs of crime's effect on employee benefits."[33] When employees realize that taking things here and there has an effect on them and their fellow employees, they will be less likely to rationalize their behavior and will begin to view their actions as actual theft.

A company that educates its employees on the effects of internal theft and that maintains a sound, caring organizational climate is going to keep its honest employees honest. According to Ben Guffey, "the majority of people are honest. The main thing you have to do is create a climate of fairness and honesty. Send your people a clear message that while temptation is normal, honesty is normal too, and the normal person won't steal."[34]

USING INTERNAL CONTROLS

Just as well-established, well-tended grass lawn makes it difficult for unwanted weeds to make inroads, so a well-run, tightly-controlled business tends to make it difficult for a dishonest employee to flourish.[35]

Given the opportunity, even an honest employee may be tempted to steal. Although establishing the right climate and the right values and beliefs will reduce the likelihood of internal theft, alone they are not sufficient to solve the problem in most businesses that employ people who possess a wide range of values. By implementing appropriate controls, theft can be reduced significantly. The point was made previously that too much control in the workplace has a negative effect on employee morale. It is apparent, however, that "when there is little opportunity to steal, even the employee with the lowest level of integrity will find it difficult to do so."[36] Loose controls in a firm without strong values and beliefs against stealing will result in increased employee theft. On the other hand, tight controls in a business with strong values and beliefs against stealing will be viewed as excessive and could result in decreased productivity. Finding the appropriate level of internal control, therefore, is a critical management job that requires good judgment.

Physical Controls

Appropriate internal controls reduce the opportunity to steal, and they are essential in a well-run business. One small business owner says, "Excellent controls are imperative." He goes on to say that "with the advent of the personal computer, the smallest of businesses can have [tight internal controls]."

Inventory management is an effective means of reducing employee theft. A company with a tightly run inventory system will be able to monitor its preventable losses and, therefore, should be able to control them. Delegating financial duties can be a useful preventive tool as well. "In an effective organization, responsibilities will be divided so that no person acting by himself can circumvent the system."[37] If access to assets can be segregated from access to accounting records, the opportunity to tamper with figures can be reduced significantly.

Other, more complex physical security measures include video monitoring, security checkpoints, and routine polygraph tests. When used alone, these security interventions can cause employee resentment.[38] This fact should never be forgotten.

Social Controls

Allowing employees to participate in the development, implementation, and monitoring of solutions to the theft problem is a form of social control, and social controls have been said to be more important in preventing employee theft than physical ones. Whatever form controls may take after employees and owners and managers have agreed on what they should be, the likelihood of success is improved. Ron Ryan, program specialist with Train-a-Vision in Fort Lee, Florida, sums it up this way: "Employees will resist efforts geared toward detection but support prevention programs. . . . [They] will more readily accept and act upon conclusions they reach themselves than upon the conclusions of others."[39] A study conducted by Richard Hollinger and John Clark suggested that "social controls, not physical controls, are in the long run the best deterrents to theft and deviance in the organization."[40]

PROSECUTION

> The amount of theft within an organization is inversely proportional to the perceived chances of getting caught.[41]

The final step in reducing employee theft is prosecution. To avoid undercutting all other prevention measures, whether they be management of organizational climate, internal controls, or prescreening measures, managers must be willing to prosecute employees who have been caught stealing. To do otherwise sends mixed signals to employees, causing confusion and frustration. There is honor among thieves, and organizations that offer safety for thieves while they practice their craft are like magnets that attract more thieves. Prosecution is the most powerful weapon you have to send the message that *theft will not be tolerated* and that thieves need not apply.

Do Not Ignore the Problem

The most important thing is that top management not sweep anything under the rug.[42]

The single greatest mistake a company can make when faced with internal theft is to delay responding to the problem. Yet many managers will not acknowledge the problem when it occurs. They either ignore it or handle it themselves for a variety of reasons. Many owners and managers believe that reporting thefts will have a negative effect on the way their firms are perceived by their customers and creditors. Some managers think that reporting thefts will reflect negatively on their ability to supervise or that it will affect employee morale negatively. As a result, many thefts that are discovered go unreported. A police investigator says that "most of the time, when a business person calls in to report a theft, he won't give specifics. Usually, they want to know how involved they must get."

Not addressing the theft problem directly is a mistake. As John Kennish describes the typical situation, "the suspect employee is usually fired but not criminally prosecuted. . . . As a result, the ex-employee promptly walks down the street and is hired by yet another unsuspecting firm."[43] The police investigator referred to previously says that "you've got to have publicity of punishment," since, unlike many business owners and managers, he believes that prosecution doesn't have a negative impact on consumer attitudes. As was stated initially, employee theft is a pervasive problem in our society that threatens the profitability of many large firms and the very existence of many small firms. Failing to prosecute employees who have demonstrated that they are criminals only makes matters worse. It sends a clear message that the owners and managers are not serious about dealing with the problem.

Anyone Can Be a Thief

A complicating issue is that many managers are unwilling to believe that their employees, many of whom are friends, are stealing from them. William A. McGurn, a former FBI agent and director for security for Holmes Protection, Inc., in New York, claims that "the biggest problem [they] have in investigating a theft is that no manager wants to believe that his employee is the guilty one."[44] Although most people do not steal, anyone can be a thief. This fact should always be kept in mind.

Consistency, Not Sympathy, Is the Answer

Even when they know an employee is guilty of stealing from them, many managers give the offender another chance out of sympathy. James Walls says, "Time and again, managers sympathize with the thief's plight: he or she has kids to support, an ailing relative, and so on. They give the thief another chance. . . . Yet in the vast majority of cases, that employee will continue to steal. It worked once, so why not try again?"[45]

Gregory Arnold calls this a "misplaced sense of obligation." He says that some managers "forgive some employee thieves because they have been with the company for a long time, or they took only a few dollars, or they have been having a hard time at home, or they really are 'nice' people and are sorry about the theft."[46]

If employees believe that theft is okay or that punishment is not a certainty, then they are going to be much more inclined to steal. Furthermore, though most employees would not steal even if they thought they could get away with it, many are deterred only by the fear of punishment. Thus managers should realize that consistent prosecution is a crucial aspect of an effective theft reduction program. Employees must believe that theft will not be condoned and that violators will be punished.

CONCLUSION

Employee theft is a pervasive problem in U.S. businesses today, accounting for 30 percent or more of all business failures. Dealing with employee theft requires owners and managers to be knowledgeable, disciplined, and willing to take action. Although all employee theft cannot be eliminated, it can be significantly reduced if certain inexpensive measures are taken. Creating an organizational climate that increases employee morale is the first step in dealing with employee theft. Establishing informal and formal controls reduces further the likelihood that theft will occur. Thoroughly prescreening prospective employees is a critical component of a theft reduction program because it enables the business person to avoid hiring potential thieves at the outset. Finally, being willing to prosecute is essential; would-be thieves will think twice before stealing if they know that they will be punished if caught.

NOTES

1. William A. Formby and Vergil L. Williams, "Enhancing Profits Through Reduction of Internal Theft," *American Journal of Small Business*, 7 (July-September 1987), p. 43.

2. Harry Bacas, "To Stop a Thief," *Nation's Business*, 75 (June 1987), pp. 16–23.

3. Rod Willis, "White-collar Crime: The Threat from Within," *Management Review*, 75 (June 1986), p. 22.

4. Bacas, "To Stop a Thief," pp. 16–23.

5. Gregory B. Arnold, "Employee Theft a $40 Billion Crime," *Management World*, 14 (November 1985), p. 27.

6. Peter Bullard and Alan Resnik, "Too Many Hands in the Corporate Cookie Jar," *Sloan Management Review*, 25 (Fall 1983), p. 52.

7. William A. McGurn, "Spotting the Thieves Who Work Among Us," *Wall Street Journal*, March 7, 1988, sect. 1, p. 16, cols. 3–6.

8. A. Bequai, "Trusted Thieves," *Security Management*, 30 (September 1986), p. 83.

9. Bacas, "To Stop a Thief," p. 23.

10. "Getting the Goods on Time Thieves," The Idea Exchange, *ABA Banking Journal*, 75 (March 1983), p. 22.

11. Robert Half, "Beating the System: How Time Theft Costs $137 Billion a Year," *Personnel Journal*, 63 (October 1984), p. 80.

12. Formby and Williams, "Enhancing Profits," pp. 43–44.

13. Leonard Adam Sipes, Jr., "Tradition Takes a Twist," *Security Management*, 31 (June 1987), p. 41.

14. Bacas, "To Stop a Thief," p. 17.

15. Charles A. Sennewald, "Theft Maxims," *Security Management*, 30 (September 1986), p. 85.

16. Irving Radler, "Silent Partners: Employees Who Embezzle," *Across the Board*, 19 (March 1982), p. 73.

17. James Walls, "Preventing Employee Theft," *Management Review*, 74 (September 1985), p. 49.

18. Bacas, "To Stop a Thief," p. 20.

19. Jules Abend, "Employee Theft," *Stores*, 68 (June 1986), p. 59.

20. "Do Unto Your Employees and They May Not Do You In," *Chain Store Age Executive*, 60 (September 1984), p. 143.

21. John W. Kennish, "Prevention Starts from the Top," *Security Management*, 29 (October 1985), p. 63.

22. Roy Carter, "Employee Theft Often Appears Legitimate," *Accountancy*, 100 (July 1987), p. 76.

23. Bullard and Resnik, "Too Many Hands," p. 55.

24. Sipes, "Tradition Takes a Twist," p. 42.

25. David C. Anderson, "Job Enrichment for Vultures, Wolves, Hawks and Donkeys," review of "Cheats at Work," by Gerald Mars, *Across the Board*, 21 (January 1984), p. 56.

26. Daniel van Buren, "Retail Manager Offers Guidelines for Curtailing Theft," *Security Management*, 32 (February 1988), pp. 112–13.

27. Ibid., p. 113.

28. Kennish, "Prevention Starts from the Top," p. 62.

29. Carter, "Employee Theft," p. 77.

30. Ibid., p. 75.

31. Ibid., p. 76.

32. Ibid., p. 77.

33. William V. Pelfrey, "Keep Honest Employees Honest," *Security Management*, 28 (December 1985), p. 24.

34. Bacas, "To Stop a Thief," p. 23.

35. Radler, "Silent Partners: Employees Who Embezzle," p. 71.

36. Bequai, "Trusted Thieves," p. 53.

37. Bacas, "To Stop a Thief," p. 21.

38. Sipes, "Tradition Takes a Twist," p. 44.

39. Ron Ryan, "Balancing the Equation to Prevent Retail Losses," *Security Management*, 29 (March 1985), p. 88.

40. Bacas, "To Stop a Thief," p. 22.

41. J. T. Wells, "Unwitting Accomplices," *Training and Development Journal*, 39 (November 1985), p. 14.

42. Walls, "Preventing Employee Theft," p. 50.

43. Kennish, "Prevention Starts from the Top," p. 60.

44. McGurn, "Spotting the Thieves," p. 16.

45. Walls, "Preventing Employee Theft," pp. 48–49.

46. Arnold, "Employee Theft," p. 27.

CHAPTER 2

Do the Right Thing: A Case Study

Business owners and managers like to think that their employees are good, honest, and upstanding people, and as we said earlier, most of them are. Additionally, many employers develop friendships with many of their employees and treat them as if they were part of their extended families. The attitudes formed in this type of environment and the bonds that develop between employers and employees are good; in fact, they are vital to successful business operation.

All too frequently, however, the people responsible for running businesses allow positive feelings about their employees to interfere with their business judgment, forgetting or choosing to ignore the fact that some of their employees will steal from them. They let their guard down and become vulnerable to the genuine thieves in their midst. To prevent this from happening, owners and managers must incorporate an antitheft philosophy into their management practices, and they must send a clear message that *theft will not be tolerated*. Failure to do this can result in significant losses and even personal injury to owners and managers, employees, and innocent bystanders.

Some employees are dishonest, and prudent business people must keep this fact in mind at all times. Furthermore, they must protect themselves, their employees, and their businesses from dishonest people, and they must discipline themselves to do the right thing. Doing the right thing means that owners and managers must be on the alert to the reality that thieves may already work for them and to the possibility that they could hire another one at any time. In addition, it means they must be ready, willing, and able to deal with a theft problem immediately when it is brought to their attention.

Therefore, it is important to decide in advance what to do when a thief is apprehended. Employees who are caught stealing are likely to have what may appear at first blush to be good excuses to justify their thievery. But there can be no justification for theft, and thieves should be terminated and prosecuted with dispatch. This fact must be clear to everyone in the firm. During the heat of the moment when a thief is detected, many owners and managers will try to avoid doing the unpleasant, but necessary, job. They will even find good reasons not to do the job. For example, they may want to temper justice with mercy; they may think that they can rehabilitate the guilty party; or they may feel sorry for the thief. These are normal and compassionate human tendencies, but they cannot be allowed to influence decision making.

A colleague of ours, James J. Dowd from the McIntire School of Commerce at the University of Virginia, has developed a case series called "Acme Irrigation, Inc." that shows what can happen when owners and managers fail to use good business judgment. These cases describe a bad experience that one compassionate businessman actually encountered. It may be an extreme case, but wisdom demands that we protect our businesses from the worst case possibility. Thus the cases are included below for your consideration. All the names and locations used in the cases have been disguised.

ACME IRRIGATION, INC. (A)

On June 26, 1986, George Waters, president of Acme Irrigation, flew to Raleigh, North Carolina, to meet with Ben Arnold, the manager of the company's most successful branch. Arriving at the Raleigh office at 4:00 P.M., he was greeted by Arnold's wife, Janet, who served as bookkeeper for the office. Although happy to see Janet, his longtime friend, Waters did not forget the purpose of his visit: He had reason to believe that Arnold was embezzling small amounts of money from the branch.

Because Arnold was out of the office, Waters asked to review the branch financial records while he awaited, and Janet gladly provided them. Within the hour Waters' suspicions were confirmed; he estimated that Arnold had stolen close to $8,000.

Company History

Acme Irrigation was founded in 1947 in Culpeper, Virginia, as a distributor of irrigation systems to local farmers. The founders were careful and conservative men, more interested in guaranteeing profitability than in risking growth. For thirty years the business prospered serving the Culpeper area. In 1980 the founders retired and sold controlling interest in the firm to George Waters, a sales representative who had worked with the company for thirteen years.

Dissatisfied with Acme's limited scope, Waters saw geographical expansion as the key to reaching the company's full potential. His goal was to see Acme as the top distributor of irrigation systems not only in Virginia, but also in West Virginia and the Carolinas.

The success of Waters' expansion plan depended largely on securing exclusive contracts with Geer, Inc., an international manufacturer of top-of-the-line irrigation equipment. Geer granted seasonal contracts to only one distributor per region and renewed or canceled these contracts depending on distributor performance. Waters knew that he would have to maintain good relations with Geer to achieve his goal.

In 1982 Waters established Acme's first branch office, in Asheville, North Carolina. Encouraged by its success, Waters opened seven additional branches by June 1986. During this time, he saw his small business grow into a successful corporation, with net worth of $6 million and sales of $15 million in 1985.

The Raleigh Branch

With high demand for irrigation systems, Raleigh had long been a top prospect for a Acme branch office. In early 1986 Waters learned that Southern Irrigation, a competitor based in Chapel Hill, North Carolina, was losing its contract with Geer after a year of disappointing sales.

Waters moved quickly to establish a Raleigh branch. Because there were no available internal candidates, Waters looked for someone outside the company to manage the branch. After interviewing several applicants, he hired Ben Arnold. Arnold had grown up in the area and was well known to local farmers; in fact, he had previously worked for Southern Irrigation as a sales representative, and he enjoyed a good reputation with Geer executives. Based on its past experiences with Acme and with Arnold, Geer awarded exclusive distribution rights for the Raleigh-Durham area to the new Acme branch.

Waters and Arnold agreed that the branch office would operate out of Arnold's home. This unusual arrangement would eliminate rent expenses and guarantee twenty-four-hour customer service; in addition, Janet Arnold would provide bookkeeping and secretarial services free of charge. To compensate the Arnolds for the use of their property, Waters agreed to give Ben an unusually high base salary of $29,000 and a 2 percent commission on sales.

The branch opened in March 1986 to immediate success. Many of Arnold's former customers from Southern Irrigation brought their business to Acme because of him. In the first two months of operation, sales reached $600,000, more than double the average sales of the other branch offices in that period. With the peak buying season just beginning, sales were expected to rise even more dramatically.

Branch Operations

Although each Acme branch operated independently, the home office established policy guidelines and maintained centralized sales and accounting records. For example, each branch sent copies of all sales orders to the home office.

Customer billing was done at the branch level, and the home office expected prompt collection of all accounts receivable, especially on major sales. It was company policy for the home office to issue reminder bills to customers whose accounts were significantly overdue.

Billing Discrepancies

On June 12 one of Acme's Raleigh customers called Culpeper to complain about a recent bill he had received from the home office. He was quite upset and insisted that he had settled his account with Arnold several weeks ago. Waters dismissed the incident as a clerical error; occasional billing discrepancies were not uncommon. In the next two weeks, however, Waters received two more customer calls with similar complaints.

His concerns about the Raleigh branch mounted when his accountant casually remarked that several of Arnold's accounts remained outstanding past the company's average collection period. In checking the files from Raleigh to confirm that observation, Waters also noticed that Arnold's travel expenses were unusually high. He decided he would visit the Raleigh branch to investigate.

George Waters

Lacking a college education and formal business training, George Waters had worked long and hard for his success. His employees looked up to him for this, even as they appreciated his "down-to-earth" personal style. He was generous with them, awarding $500 bonuses to all employees at Christmas, and lenient in granting extra time off. He also was known for his tolerance and understanding, able to forgive the mistakes of others because he could well remember his own. Willie Hayden, for example, had worked for Waters for twelve years but was constantly in dire financial straits. Each Christmas, Waters gave Hayden a double bonus in the hope of helping him out of his trouble.

Ben Arnold

Ben Arnold, age thirty-five, had grown up on a large farm in Raleigh and knew almost every farmer in his part of the state. The local farmers respected his agricultural knowledge and often turned to him for advice in both business and personal matters.

Until a year ago, Arnold had commuted to Chapel Hill to work at Southern Irrigation, Acme's biggest competitor. He had held this position for ten years and had then resigned, for reasons unclear to Waters. Ben and his wife, Janet, had just begun remodeling their large farmhouse, and were expecting their first child in August.

Waters and Arnold had met for the first time more than a year ago, at the Arnolds' wedding. A guest of the bride, Waters was impressed with Arnold's expertise in the irrigation business. They discussed the idea of starting up a Acme branch in Raleigh, so when Waters later decided to open the Raleigh branch, Arnold immediately came to mind as a natural candidate for branch manager.

The Current Situation

Now, sitting in the Acme office in Arnold's home, Waters realized the truth. The billing errors were not simple clerical mistakes. Unaware that the home office would be following up on outstanding accounts, Arnold had apparently been skimming money off the top of large transactions.

As the clock struck five, Arnold's car pulled into the driveway. Waters' plane was scheduled to leave at 8:15 P.M.

ACME IRRIGATION, INC. (B)

Waters greeted Arnold as he came into the office and explained that he wanted to discuss Arnold's forecasts for the upcoming season. They made plans to meet for dinner at L & N Seafood in one hour. Waters made some phone calls and then left for the restaurant, arriving early so he could collect his thoughts. When Arnold arrived, Waters asked him to sit down and then confronted him with his suspicions. Arnold vehemently denied having stolen any money, and expressed disbelief that Waters could accuse him of such dishonesty.

When Waters threatened to telephone local farmers for clarification, Arnold admitted his guilt. He tearfully pleaded with Waters for a second chance. He explained that he was financially desperate, having incurred enormous medical bills as a result of Janet's pregnancy, while already overextended as a result of the construction on his house. He had only intended to borrow the money from the business, and he promised to pay it all back as soon as possible. He also begged Waters never to tell Janet what he had done.

Glancing at his watch, Waters noted that it was now 7:00 P.M.

ACME IRRIGATION, INC. (C)

George Waters weighed his decision carefully. What were the consequences of firing Ben Arnold?

He considered the impact on the Raleigh branch. The peak sales season had just begun, and he had anticipated extremely strong profits from the branch. Many Acme customers did business with the company only because Ben Arnold was there; how would they react if George told them Ben had been fired? Ben would describe his wife's difficult pregnancy, tell them that he had temporarily, out of desperation, borrowed money from the business—and then been fired! What would be left of Acme's reputation in the area?

Then Waters remembered his friend, Janet Arnold. How would she feel if she learned what her husband had done? Would the news cause further complications in her pregnancy? How would she and her new baby get along if Ben were fired from his job? Would she blame Waters for being too harsh?

He tried to put himself in Arnold's shoes. To what extremes would he go if his own wife's health were in danger? He had to admit he would consider borrowing money from the business to make medical payments. He remembered the high praise he had heard from area farmers for Ben Arnold, his hard work, and his honesty. If Arnold would go to such lengths to protect his wife, Waters thought, he had to be a good person at heart.

Finally, Waters looked across the table at Arnold and told him he agreed: Janet should not know. He said he understood what Arnold had done, and why he had done it. Arnold thanked him and promised that Waters would never regret his decision.

The two men then worked out a plan for Arnold to repay the money to Acme. After warning Arnold that he would be monitoring the Raleigh branch very closely, Waters stood, shook hands, and left for the airport.

It would be difficult to argue with the fact that George Waters is a compassionate man and that Ben Arnold is fortunate. Ben has been given a second chance, and George probably feels like he has been a true friend to both Janet and Ben. But what has George actually done, and why did he do it? These questions are important, and answering them should make it easier for us to understand why theft is such a difficult problem to solve for many people.

Friendship

George has known Janet since he was a boy, and he considers her a true friend. He would not want to do anything to hurt her. Now that she is married to Ben, anything that hurts him, in George's opinion, will hurt her. Furthermore, Janet is experiencing a difficult pregnancy, and additional stress at this time could complicate her condition. Because he is Janet's friend, George decides not to press charges and to keep Ben's theft a secret from Janet. To George, this seems like a reasonable decision, especially since Ben is going to pay the money back anyway.

But what has George actually done, and how does Ben interpret

George's compassion? Ben might be thankful and fulfill his promise to repay the money and never steal again. On the other hand, he may be a true thief and interpret George's behavior as weakness. In which case, he believes that George will tolerate theft, and he will steal again. Only time will tell whether George did the right thing.

Ready, Willing, and Able

Ben's theft caught George by surprise. He had never seriously considered the possibility that Ben would steal from him, so he was not prepared for it. You could tell from his actions that George did not know what to do. After he looked at the records and knew Ben was stealing, he was forced to devise a plan to deal with the problem spontaneously. George's idea was to meet Ben at a local restaurant and decide what to do during the meeting. At the very least, he could have decided beforehand what his options were and the conditions under which each one would be used. For example, he could fire Ben for stealing, fire and prosecute Ben, ask for Ben's resignation and demand restitution, or retain Ben and demand restitution.

Without giving the decision the careful attention it deserved, George decided to use the last option mentioned. This "seat of the pants" approach seldom produces good results. In fact, it has about as much chance of succeeding as the odds of a baseball player getting a hit when he swings the bat with his eyes closed. This decision approach leaves too much to chance, and it sacrifices most of the control George might have had in this situation. Nonetheless, George decided to retain Ben and demand restitution. But, not having thought the problem through, George was not ready, willing, or able to deal with the problem when Ben entered the restaurant. This oversight was definitely not good business.

Excuses

George probably expected Ben to deny stealing the money. It makes sense that if Ben had stolen the money, he would never have admitted guilt on the basis of an accusation alone. Thus George was prepared to present the facts proving Ben's guilt, and he did. The facts showed beyond a shadow of a doubt that Ben was guilty. It was not a marginal case or a close call. It was out-and-out theft, and Ben knew it as well as anyone.

When George presented the facts, Ben broke down, cried, and pleaded for mercy. This behavior is not surprising either, but George's strategy broke down at this point. Ben had been caught red-handed. George could have figured out in advance what Ben would do when accused, and he could have prepared for the inevitable result. It was simple. Ben would do anything he could at that point to minimize the consequences of his actions. What choice did he have but to plead for compassion, understanding, and mercy?

Ben was possibly the most surprised person in the restaurant when George agreed to overlook the incident if Ben would make restitution. It seems natural for a thief to expect severer punishment when apprehended than Ben received. Furthermore, Ben must have understood that George was reluctant to deal with him objectively because of George's feelings for Janet. Thus we contend that Ben felt safe at this point and that the odds of his having a serious change of heart because of this encounter were slim. In other words, Ben would steal again. Why should he change? He was not punished. He only had a close call.

Good Intentions Can Result in Bad Decisions

George's intentions were laudable. He wanted to help Janet, and he felt sorry for Ben. Most of all, he desperately wanted to believe Ben. Maybe Ben really did intend to pay back the money. But if he intended to pay back the money, why did he not ask for a loan or for an advance? George might have thought about the similarity between taking money out of petty cash and replacing it with an IOU and borrowing from cash flow. There are similarities, but Ben did not put in an IOU to cover himself.

Ben must have known that he eventually would be found out. How could he take thousands of dollars and expect no one to complain? If he honestly saw the money he was taking as a loan, then he would have made certain to leave a paper trail showing evidence of that fact. Instead, he did nothing. Thus, at the very least, George should have concluded that Ben was incapable of handling money, and he immediately should have taken steps to make certain that Ben would not be tempted by cash again. Not taking adequate precautionary steps to prevent the same problem from arising again was one of George's major mistakes. George's good intentions were preventing him from doing the right thing.

ACME IRRIGATION, INC. (D)

For the next ten weeks it seemed that everything had worked out extremely well. Sales for the Raleigh branch exceeded all forecasts, and on August 3 Janet gave birth to a healthy baby girl. Waters was convinced that he had done the right thing.

Then a customer from Raleigh called the home office to complain about a bill he had received. He had been credited with a payment of only $4,500 on a $12,000 system for which he had paid in full. Waters assured the man that the bill was a mistake, and he promised to resolve it personally.

Alarmed, Waters immediately called the bank in Raleigh. He learned that Arnold had cashed the customer's check for $12,000 and deposited $4,500.

Waters tried several times but could not reach Arnold by phone until 8:00 that night. Furious, he demanded to know what Arnold had done with the customer's money. Arnold said he couldn't speak then because Janet was in the room, mentioned a large bill he had to pay immediately for the business, and then hung up. Convinced that Arnold had stolen the money, Waters immediately called four employees and asked them to meet him at the Culpeper office at 5:00 the next morning.

They drove to Arnold's home but found no one there. They loaded all the Acme equipment onto their trucks, though Waters could not find many of the machines and tools that Arnold had borrowed from the home office.

He began calling customers the next day, assuring them that their Acme systems would be serviced by another office, and informing them that the Raleigh branch had been closed for reasons he could not discuss.

That afternoon he received a call from Ben Arnold. He told Waters that he was sorry things hadn't worked out, but he couldn't understand why Waters had collected all the equipment so suddenly. When Waters asked what Arnold had told Janet, Arnold hung up.

Waters worked with his lawyer and his accountant to determine the full measure of Arnold's theft. Including cash and equipment, Arnold had stolen more than $27,000. Waters vowed to recover his losses in court, and he resolved that he would tell Janet the truth about her husband.

Six days later George heard from Janet's mother that Janet had been in a terrible accident and was not expected to live. He went to Raleigh and was met at the hospital by Janet's parents and Arnold, who acted as though nothing had happened between them. Arnold claimed that Janet, who had been emotionally unstable ever since the birth of their daughter, had become hysterical and suddenly jumped out of his truck while they were driving forty-five miles an hour down a back road. Knowing Arnold to be a liar, and knowing Janet as he did, Waters doubted the story but remained silent, given the gravity of the situation.

Janet remained in a coma for eight months. When she finally recovered, it took another four months before she could speak even simple phrases. Slowly, she was able to recall what had happened.

Having discovered that her husband was heavily involved with drugs, she confronted him. When she told him she would take their daughter and leave him if he didn't get some help, he struck her and knocked her out. When she awoke, she was riding in the truck with him. She pleaded with him to talk to her, but he refused. Then, out on a back road, he reached over, pulled the door handle, and pushed her out.

Janet went to the police, but they were unable to prosecute because they had no evidence to corroborate her story. She sued for divorce, won custody of her daughter, and moved back to Culpeper to live with her parents, where she sees George Waters from time to time. Neither has ever heard from Ben Arnold again.

George might have prevented this terrible ordeal. What would have happened if he had not been so compassionate earlier? At the very least, Ben's wrongdoing would have been exposed to the light of day, and Janet would have known that something was wrong. Janet's knowing the facts might not have prevented the tragic series of events from occurring later, but it might have.

This much we can say with certainty: No one involved in these cases would have been any worse off if George had done the right thing earlier. George would have lost less money, and his firm's reputation would have been less tarnished. Janet might have avoided being beaten up by Ben if she had known about his drug problem. Ben might have been forced to come to grips with his problem and deal with it. It is possible that George, Janet, the baby, Janet's family, and Ben would all have been better off if George had simply done the right thing.

CHAPTER 3

Employee Theft from Two Perspectives

As we developed our strategy for reducing employee theft, we contacted, or were contacted by, several groups and individuals who were interested in some aspect of the problem. From them we learned a great deal about employee theft and about the reasons people steal.

Roger Self, a partner in a business called Southeastern Loss Management, Inc., in Gastonia, North Carolina, read about our work in the Gastonia newspaper and called us to find out exactly what we were doing and how we got started. As we got to know Roger, we realized that he had accumulated a wealth of knowledge and experience during many years of work in loss prevention. In particular, Roger was intrigued by people's motives for stealing. His was not an academic interest limited to psychological problems that might cause some people to steal, but rather he was concerned about real-world problems people encounter daily that can result in employee theft.

We asked Roger to share his knowledge and experience with us, and we have included it here for your consideration. Below Roger discusses his background and his views on employees who steal from their employers.

AN INVESTIGATOR'S PERSPECTIVE

I became interested in the subject of theft before I graduated from high school. One evening after school I discovered that my car had been broken into and all of my audiotapes were missing. I valued these tapes, and I wanted them back. The person who stole the tapes must have been in a hurry because he left a cardboard box in the car that contained a brown and white pet rabbit.

By the end of the day I had recovered my tapes, returned a stolen rabbit to a local pet store, and gotten confessions from two thieves. People might think what I did was strange or unusual, but I solved this case simply by being aware of the things around me and by paying careful attention to the evidence at hand. In this case, I used good old common sense as well. For example, I was aware that many students skipped school and went to the local mall to "hang out." It just so happened that the only pet store in the county at the time was in the mall. Thus I took my high school annual and the rabbit to the pet store.

When I entered the pet store with the stolen rabbit, the manager was amazed. He told me that two high school–aged boys were in the pet store earlier in the day at about lunch, and that they often visited his store at that time. I asked him to look through my annual to identify the boys, and he was delighted to do it. Fortunately, he recognized both of them, and I was on my way to recovering the tapes. Later that evening I visited one of the boys at home, and he admitted to stealing my tapes. He returned them to me, and I agreed not to report the incident to the police.

This was my first experience dealing directly with theft, and, I must tell you, I enjoyed it. Solving the crime was exciting and challenging, and it required me to use my logic and my wits. As it turned out, I became so interested in crime detection and prevention that I became a city police patrolman after graduating from high school.

I really enjoyed the thought of working for the police department, and at first I looked forward to my job every day. That attitude did not last long, however, because of the way policemen were trained at the time. You see, rookie police officers were given the job of walking the beat on Main Street to "break them in."

Walking the beat bored me to death, so to make things interesting I would visit retail establishments and watch for shoplifters. I can remember going into a drugstore and looking for shoplifters while wearing a police uniform. Now that was difficult, but after I found an inconspicuous place from which I could see the customers in the store, I learned a great deal. For example, I learned that the trick to catching shoplifters is to pay attention to the behavior of honest customers. There are several differences between the way honest people and shoplifters act in a store, but the most obvious difference is the look in their eyes. I will say more about how to identify suspects later.

When I was promoted from "the beat" to a patrol car, my fascination with theft continued. I would drive to the local retail centers and malls and watch the parking lots as customers pulled in and out. On one occasion I observed a man and a woman pull up near the entrance of a J. C. Penney store. The man remained in the car while the woman hurried inside the store. Just before she entered, she looked back at the man in an odd way. Less than five minutes later she hurriedly came out carrying a large bag stuffed full of merchandise. Just by being observant and by noticing that the bag she was carrying had not been packed neatly, the way a store employee would have packed it, I surmised that she had stolen the merchandise. My suspicion was confirmed after I approached her and asked to see her receipt. This experience reconfirmed a simple truth: If you pay attention to the details, you will learn that most thieves telegraph their intentions and their actions. You just have to pay attention.

After spending five years in police work, I moved into retailing and quickly learned about internal, or employee, theft. I headed a small loss prevention department in a 200,000-square-foot retail department store that in the past had concentrated on apprehending shoplifters. It did not take me long to realize that many employees were stealing from the company, so I spent some time developing a program to deal with the problem. Almost immediately I identified my first employee theft case. It resulted in an internal investigation that uncovered a theft ring involving ten employees. The group had worked together for a few months and had been able to embezzle more than $10,000.

Since handling that case I have been involved in more than 200 employee theft investigations ranging from the theft of candy and soft drinks to the embezzlement of large amounts of cash. I have made it a practice in each of these cases to interview the thieves in depth and to make sure I understood what they were doing and why they did it. In the process, I have learned a great deal about employee theft. I will share some of what I have learned from my experiences.

First, an employer must realize that most employees who steal send signals that I call *employee theft indicators,* and they leave behind evidence of their larceny that can be used to identify the guilty party or parties. Employee theft indicators are not violations of the law; they are merely indicators of possible employee theft. Because of their proximity, some owners and managers may not be in a position to observe and respond to these indicators. Therefore, it is essential for every business to elevate loss prevention to a high level of importance and to make certain that every person in the organization with supervisory responsibility, from top to bottom, understands and adheres to the company's loss prevention program.

One of the most common indicators of employee theft is an unwillingness to make eye contact. I have found from experience that the way employees look at you and at others says a lot about their honesty, or lack of it. Many people may disagree, but I have based this conclusion on many years of hard work and experience. For example, I have watched employees who are in the act of stealing, and just before they take something they almost always look around to see who else is in the area or if anyone else is watching. Furthermore, they tend to look away quickly if they see you are watching them, or they appear visibly shaken because of your presence. In addition, I have seen employees take cash out of cash registers while they stood near the register pretending to be daydreaming. It is almost uncanny how consistently you can detect employee theft by just watching the movement of the eye. I have watched employees steal while they were being recorded on closed-circuit television (CCTV), and about 98 percent of the time they look around in an unusual way before the theft occurs. If you witness these behaviors in some of your employees, you may have problems.

Sudden movements are almost as revealing as the lack of eye contact. Many times I have walked up on employees while they were in the act of stealing only to have them move quickly in an awkward way and then look back at me with a blank look on their faces. I was once walking through a department and observed a salesclerk talking with a prominent city official. When the clerk saw me (she knew that I was the security manager), her entire facial expression changed, as if she was shocked to see me. I asked the CCTV operator to watch them. The city official quickly left the store, so I instructed the CCTV operator to keep an eye on the salesclerk until she got off work. About four hours later the city official returned and participated in an embezzlement of merchandise from the store. The clerk gave the official more than $100 in merchandise for $5. It was the sudden movement that caused me to watch these people closely, and they are the indicators that resulted in their being caught. No one would ever have suspected these two persons, especially the city official, of participating in a scheme like this one.

Lying is another theft indicator. An employee who is willing to lie is likely to be willing to steal as well. Lying is closely related to stealing. The person who will lie to you is already dishonest in at least one important respect. Many times after an investigation has been completed, I learn that the thief lied a lot too. I have learned to keep my eyes on the people who lie routinely. Every owner or manager I have worked with can tell me about the many problems they have had over the years with employees who are chronic liars. My advice to them is to watch these people carefully.

Overly friendly behavior is a theft indicator in some instances. I want to be careful here because some people are simply friendly and have outgoing personalities. Not only are they a pleasure to work with, but they influence the attitudes of their co-workers positively. Nonetheless, I always advise my clients to keep in mind that employees who steal need a cover and that counterfeit friendship is a great cover. When employee theft occurs, owners and managers tend to ignore their good, loyal, long-term employees as possible culprits because they cannot believe that these people would steal from them. But the evidence is clear that these employees can steal, and that is because they are liked so much they can get away with more than the ordinary thief could. Thus I recommend showing no favoritism in a theft investigation. This policy has worked well over the years.

Frequent sickness or calling in sick just after a theft has occurred may be suspicious. For example, one of my clients experienced a recurrent cash shortage problem, and he called me in to investigate. The thefts occurred at about three-day intervals, and my first step in the investigation was to chart the work schedules of all the employees. As I made my charts, I noticed that one employee was out of work because of sickness immediately after each shortage. I interviewed her about the thefts, and she confessed. Interestingly, she told me she knew stealing was wrong and that she always had stomach trouble after she stole. Evidently her stomachaches were a psychosomatic response to her behavior. At first I thought it was odd, but my experience has taught me that it is not uncommon for people who steal to actually become physically ill afterward. I also have found that many employees who steal just like to take some time off after the crime, so they call in sick.

There is an array of other psychological problems that can cause people to steal, even though they do not need the money. I have conducted numerous investigations that uncovered thieves who were financially secure and had good reputations. Interviewing them, I learned that problems like difficulty communicating with parents, a death in the family, loneliness, divorce, or depression are at the root of many cases of employee theft. For example, one young lady had lost both her mother and her father in an automobile accident, and she was later caught stealing. She did not need the money because her parents had left her financially secure. But she stole anyway and could not explain why. She told me she had never stolen anything before her parents died, and I am confident that she was telling me the truth. Evidently the trauma associated with the accident triggered something that caused her to behave differently.

Although teenaged kids have always been vulnerable to peer pressure, it is worse today than it was in the past. In particular, theft owing to peer pressure is on the rise. I cannot tell you how many times I have conducted investigations and found that the guilty party was a high school student who was trying to impress his or her friends. Many of the young people I have caught stealing simply give merchandise to, or they discount merchandise for, their friends. Once I caught a teenaged girl giving away sixteen pairs of $80 shoes, so she would be accepted. I caught a high school boy giving away a swimsuit and jeans to a young girl whose name he did not even know just so he could impress her. He said that he was trying to get to know her better.

Today's young people are not as well grounded in traditional values as they once were. In the past the kids who stole knew what they were doing was wrong, but they went ahead and did it anyway. Today many young people do not think stealing is wrong. If you talk with owners and managers of fast-food restaurants that employ large numbers of young people, most of them will confirm this conclusion. For this reason, I think employee theft will continue to increase for many more years.

In most cases employees leave evidence of theft that often is overlooked by management, and there are a variety of fraudulent practices that can be detected and should be monitored closely. For example, refund fraud is a problem I frequently have encountered that employees can use by circumventing—quite easily I should add—company policies to obtain cash for themselves. This is done by making up fictitious customers and writing up refunds for them, and then taking the cash.

One time I caught two long-term, apparently loyal employees using this scheme. Their plan worked like this. The company required the signatures of two salesclerks to obtain a refund. One was required to fill out the refund ticket, and the other was supposed to see the customer and merchandise before approving the refund. The two salesclerks in question were close friends, and they worked together to satisfy the company's policy. Fortunately for the store owner, these thieves used the names of people from the phone book on the refund tickets. During a routine audit of refunds, two customers told me that they had never shopped at the store. After questioning both clerks, they admitted to taking more than $3,000 in fraudulent refunds. If they had chosen to use fictitious names instead, the owner would have had much more difficulty. Most frauds committed through the refund system can be prevented by closely auditing all refunds frequently. Management can call or write customers who obtain refunds, asking for customer service information. This is a simple solution, but it is not used very often by many store owners.

Fraud may occur in many other ways as well. Thus a wise owner or manager of a business would be well advised to keep a watchful eye on all documents created by employees, such as voided sales, invoices and manifests. I once caught a young man who took about $3,000 by voiding sales. Also, I discovered a truck driver who was allowed to fill out his own orders, and after loading his own truck, he would change the written order to show less merchandise on his truck than was actually on it. This man stole many thousands of dollars before he was caught.

Time card fraud is extremely common in business today, and it should be monitored closely too. Employees will occasionally check one another in and/or out to show more hours worked than were actually worked. Time card fraud is easy to prevent. It can be done by checking times or sign-in sheets against the actual times employees work, but not many owners or managers pay much attention to the problem.

By keeping track of voids, overrings, refunds, and so on, managers can detect patterns that will reveal normal levels of transactions in each of these areas and in departments. These records also will show how the patterns of transaction levels change during the year. Once this information is collected, any significant variations should be investigated immediately. For example, if the average number of voids or refunds per employee in a week is twenty-five, and you have an employee who does twenty-five per day, you may have a problem.

Several important ideas that will help to reduce employee theft are listed below.

1. The most important step to reduce employee theft is management awareness and involvement. Management and supervisory personnel must make loss prevention a priority, and they must never allow themselves to be tempted to steal or to do anything that even resembles stealing. Managers need to set the example for others to follow.

2. Creative employees will find ways to steal if they want to do it, and they can always find ways to work around any company policies. I have discovered that education concerning loss prevention and employee involvement is one of the best methods for reducing employee theft. Unfortunately, only rarely have I come across people in business who talk with their employees about stealing, but I cannot overemphasize the importance of doing it. Don't assume your employees see the world the way you do.

3. Furthermore, most internal thefts can be prevented, but theft reduction requires an investment in training for owners, managers, and employees. Unless this step is taken, theft will continue to be a significant problem. Education and continuous training are the key to reducing all types of theft. Controls and policies also are important; however, if employees are not constantly reminded of losses, these and other reduction strategies and approaches will not work. Every company I have ever worked with had written security policies and procedures, but they did not prevent employee theft.

4. Theft reduction programs do not have to be expensive or time-consuming to be effective. A cost-effective program can be designed if the following recommendations are implemented:

   a. Appoint a committee to look at the theft issue that includes people from every level, department, or area.

   b. Have regular monthly meetings to discuss loss prevention.

   c. Set up a confidential employee hot line for employees to report dishonest actions.

   d. Show employees who have reported thefts that you appreciate what they have done. Some firms award bonuses to employees who report theft, and that approach has worked well.

   e. Prescreening of job applicants is critical, and time should be taken to do this job properly.

   f. Managers must be alert to the many ways employees can steal from the company, and they must carefully and regularly monitor areas where they are vulnerable.

   g. Keep records of any suspicious activities. Good records reveal patterns that are important indicators of employee theft.

   h. Catch employees doing things right too. It is important for owners and managers to provide positive reinforcement for employees who are contributing to the success of the business. If you do not provide positive reinforcement, many employees will get it in less constructive and less profitable ways, and some of them will steal if you do not provide it.

i. Change your daily, monthly, quarterly, and yearly routines regularly. When thieves know your routines, they have the upper hand because they can accurately anticipate your actions. You would like to be predictable most of the time on most important issues, but employees should not be able to anticipate audits and spot checks easily.

j. Always remember that it only takes a few minutes of your time, in most cases, to prevent employee theft.

k. It takes two conditions for theft to occur: opportunity and need. We cannot always affect an employee's need to steal, but we are in control of the opportunities they have to steal.

Interviewing employees you suspect are stealing requires discipline and patience. The most important thing to remember when you are interviewing an employee you suspect is stealing is not to violate his or her legal rights. Do not accuse any employee of any wrongdoing unless and until you are prepared to prove that a crime has been committed. If you believe that you have enough circumstantial evidence and want to question an employee, remember these suggestions:

1. Make sure you conduct the interview in a private place where you cannot be disturbed by any interruption, including the telephone.

2. Let the employee know that you want to discuss a serious matter that needs immediate attention.

3. Ensure complete confidentiality.

4. Your most effective tool is a courteous, fair attitude. You will get much better information from a suspect by being courteous and polite than by being authoritative or abusive.

5. Explain to the suspect that you have obtained information but do not reveal how, where, or from whom you got it.

6. Advise the suspect that you are only gathering information at this point on a completely confidential basis.

7. If you do not intend to pursue criminal prosecution, advise the suspect that any information gathered will be handled completely in house and will not be given to any outside authorities. Assure the suspect that if you receive full cooperation, the matter will be handled in confidence and in house. Under no circumstances should you violate your word!

Interviewing suspected thieves is serious business. You must have enough circumstantial evidence to justify an interview before you begin questioning the suspect. If you have any doubts whatsoever about anything, you should contact a professional investigator. However, if you believe that you have good information pointing to the suspect, then follow the guidelines presented above.

THE PERSPECTIVE OF A WOMAN WHO WAS
CONVICTED FOR EMBEZZLEMENT

Donna Beitel grew up in Wheaton, Illinois. She is a mother of three adult children, and she has a story to tell that owners and managers of businesses need to hear. Donna began her career by starting a small secretarial business in her home. She did good work, and was drafted by a local attorney to work for him full time as his secretary. Shortly thereafter she became involved in politics in Oswego, serving for eight years as the village treasurer. Donna held offices in several professional associations at the state and federal levels, and she was what you would call a very professional, dependable, trustworthy woman.

In 1985 Donna was indicted on embezzlement charges in connection with funds missing in the village of Oswego. She subsequently was convicted, and served a sentence with the Illinois Department of Corrections. Below is a message Donna wanted to share with the readers of this book.

I became an expert on employee theft and white-collar crime the hard way— by letting myself get involved in an embezzlement scheme. I've made some really bad choices in my life—choices that nearly took my life from me. I have paid dearly for those mistakes, and through my company, Interventions, I have embarked on an all-out effort to prevent other people from making the same kinds of mistakes.

Having spent a full year in the prison system, I came out determined to use my experience for the benefit of others. I searched for over a year before I came upon a way that would work for me. I now spend my time giving lectures and workshops, and have been quite successful in raising the general level of awareness about the problem. Too often people simply refuse to recognize how widespread the problem is—and that it has (or will) touch nearly everyone's life in one way or another.

In addition to lecturing, I work with people accused of these crimes and I work with their families. Because of my personal experience, I have found that I am able to relate to these people on a deeper level—and they feel free to really open up to me. I have a very strong faith in God and, through my church, have learned new ways to help others deal with the resulting crisis. I have also gone directly into prisons to talk with the inmates about rebuilding their lives, and know in my heart that I have been an inspiration to several of them.

I also do private consultations for businesses. I have jokingly said that I can go into the accounting department of any business for thirty days and come out telling the management at least two ways to take $10,000. Well, it turned out to be not so much of a joke because I have done exactly that on more than one occasion. That can really open someone's eyes to the weaknesses in their system.

My goal is to open your eyes—to make you see just how widespread and how common white-collar crime is. I also hope to open your hearts—to give you a glimpse inside the life of a real white-collar criminal. I have yet to discuss this subject with someone who has never been affected by white-collar crime in one way or another—everyone seems to know someone who was involved, either as an offender or as a victim: your neighbor, your cousin, the man down the street, your boss.

You could almost say white-collar crime does pay. The benefits are immediate, it is difficult to detect, and the victims are reluctant to prosecute. The average embezzler can keep his game going for years before he makes that one big mistake that blows everything wide open—and even then he can expect an administrative slap on the wrist, the loss of his job, perhaps some bad newspaper coverage—but rarely can he expect prosecution through the courts. Society is focusing on street crimes—crimes that hurt people. The white-collar criminal is usually very careful not to hurt anyone.

Certainly the most difficult part for me in being caught in this type of crime was having to admit to my family that I really did do something so wrong. By working to prevent these things from occurring in the first place, I can perhaps save a few families from that shock.

So ... how did I steal? It was so simple that for six years no one thought to look, and when they did, it took two years for them to believe I could be so dumb. Dumb also got me a year in prison and a personal life that was torn to pieces. As a public official, I was subject to a certified public audit each and every year. In spite of what I was doing "behind the scenes," I managed to pass the audit tests each and every year. During my years of embezzlement, I became somewhat prominent in the field of finance administration, and quite active in professional associations, holding offices at both state and national levels. By the time I realized how much I liked the profession I had chosen, I was in so far that it was impossible to straighten things out. There was no place to go but deeper.

Put into simple terms, I played the float and altered bank statements to cover my activity. I knew that my certified audit would be a "photograph" of the financial situation of my city on the same date each year. Because of the sheer volume of money involved, it was relatively easy for me to use a variety of methods to make it appear that funds were in more than one place at the same time each year when my audit "photo" was snapped. During the year, whenever I felt a need to properly compensate myself for the excellent job I was doing (we'll explore that attitude later), I simply wrote myself a check from the general, co-mingled checking account.

Why did I steal? For the same reason most white-collar criminals get involved—and greed has almost nothing to do with it. The average white-collar criminal sees himself as very much abused by his employer, and I was no exception. I had done some really great things from my desk at City Hall. I had taken an almost useless investment program and turned it into one that was both aggressive and fruitful. Interest earned during my first year in office was more than 600 percent of that earned the year before. For this effort I was never even acknowledged, even though I pointed out my accomplishment to my governing board. As chairman of the city's Personnel Committee, I was asked to come up with a comprehensive personnel policy. After many long months of research, committee meetings, and typing, I had a policy that was so good it was later used as a model by other cities of our size. That accomplishment was barely recognized either. I felt very strongly about the "great things" I was doing, things that directly benefitted both the elected officials and the taxpayers in general. For all I accomplished during my first term in office, I was given a salary increase that amounted to little more than 5 cents an hour. I was still earning less than the average file clerk in a private office. Of course, I said, "Poor me."

I also had the problem of travel to deal with. I was encouraged to become active in political and professional associations and found it was "my cup of tea." Here I was able to "bloom." I had found a group of people who really did appreciate my accomplishments. We were all in the same boat and served as real support persons for each other. I so needed the "approval" that I received from my co-professionals that I wanted to attend every meeting that was scheduled, and not just those meetings in my home state. I felt the need to go national as well. My travel budget at City Hall was very tight, and my personal resources already strained. It seemed only logical that I should find a way for the city to cover this expense. After all, it was because of the city that I was involved with these groups. And it was because of me that the city had all that extra income to spare. In fact, one sweet person who defended my actions said, "I don't know what you are complaining about; they still have much more money than they would have if you had never worked there." The problem was, of course, that earning the money didn't make it mine for the taking—a lesson I learned the hard way!

I clearly remember the first time I actually wrote myself a city check. It was going to be just a loan till payday. Oh, how many times I've heard that! I don't remember just what the problem was, but I knew this "loan" would straighten it out. "Just a loan," I kept telling myself. By the time payday got there, the bank statement had already arrived, and I managed to dummy up a reconciliation that no one questioned. That "loan" was never repaid and the situation grew continually worse.

In time, I came to see the little withdrawals as a way to compensate myself for all that I had to tolerate and to correct the inadequacy in my salary. I always intended to put it back but never quite came up with the extra cash. At one point, about two years into my problem, I realized that I was doing something seriously wrong. I went to an attorney and told him the whole story, pleading for help in getting out of the mess I had made. I was at a point where I could have still borrowed enough money to straighten out the city books, and had resigned myself to the fact that I would have to tell my husband about everything. But my attorney's advice was not what I expected, and it cost me dearly. "This is politics, my dear... smile at them and try to put it back." He inadvertently affirmed my notion that what I was doing was not so bad after all. I did manage to replace a few hundred dollars, but as time went on and I continued to avoid detection, it turned into sort of a challenge to continue getting away with it. Soon I was making "withdrawals" on a regular basis, and never even considered the possibility that I might get caught. As with most white-collar criminals, I felt invincible—and I felt justified.

So how does a person of normally high values live with the knowledge that he is doing something profoundly wrong? I found a way to "block out" the reality of my wrongdoing. I simply didn't think about it except just before audit each year. I took regular vacations and rarely worried about what was going on at City Hall while I was gone. I simply did not acknowledge to myself that I was involved... and the covering-up was just another part of my monthly bookkeeping routine.

Then there was the day I thought my world had exploded. I was told there was a "discrepancy" in the books, and I would be temporarily suspended from my duties until it was resolved. I had never been so frightened in my entire life—not so much of the legal consequences if I had indeed been caught, but of having to tell my family what I had done. In spite of the incredible pain I caused them, they found it in their hearts to forgive me (and my wonderful husband even managed to justify my actions in his own mind). My husband did not leave me, as I was certain he would. He stood by me through nine months of messy court proceedings and bad newspaper coverage.

My mistake was made in a small town, and small towns have a quality all their own. There is a true saying about a small town: "It is a place where everyone knows if their check is good and your wife isn't." The entire ordeal turned into a witch hunt of sorts—with me as the subject. I can still hardly believe it actually happened. I eventually pleaded guilty to charges brought against me and was sentenced to two and one-half years in prison. And, incredibly, I was totally relieved that my years of deception were finally over. It was like the weight of the world was lifted off my shoulders—like I could finally breathe again.

I was released from prison after one year, and I am thankful to be one of the fortunate few who managed to survive an ordeal of this type. The strength of my family, my faith in God, and the love of some very special friends pulled me through. I won't turn "Sunday sermon" on you here, but there is something I need to say about God. God is part of my life now. I thank Him every day for the guidance he gives me. We chose to stay in the small town where I committed my crime. I make regular restitution payments to the city, and the citizens of that town have accepted us again as friends and neighbors. As a result of my experience, I have become determined to spread the word and find ways to stop others from making the same mistakes I did.

Who can say they never took home an extra pen or two, or a box of paper clips, or a copy of some software? Not many of us. It would be terribly wrong to cross the street and steal from your neighbor, but it somehow doesn't seem so wrong to take something home with us from our own place of employment. White-collar crime is not a whole new book; it is just the next page.

I have put together a profile of the employer who is likely to have an embezzlement problem. Most companies' standards are set by the boss—he must never think that the employees don't know what he is doing. If he is just a manager, he may fudge on his expense account, but if he owns the company, he is apt to be much more possessive about profits. Specifically, this boss who sets the wrong example may:

1. Put his own family on the company payroll, though they never come to work
2. Throw a cash receipt into his pocket rather than into the company books
3. Have company vehicles that are never seen or used by the company business, or
4. Send his personal bills through company books for payment

A work environment that includes a general attitude of honesty and trust, among management and employees alike, will promote that very same thing. If there is an office slush fund (and there normally is), there is less respect for the idea of accounting for our actions. Rather than permitting the existence of that slush fund, an employer might loosen up his policy for reimbursing petty cash expenses to his employees. If someone gets what they think they are entitled to above board, there is no reason to go after it any other way.

What are some of the specific actions that an employer can take to lessen his chances of being hit with a white-collar crime?

1. First and foremost, he can set a good example. If he needs $2,000 a month to pay his country club bill, by all means take it (he is entitled to any and all profits of his own business)—but take it as a salary increase or as a monthly bonus that goes through payroll or the owner's draw account. If part of that country club bill is a business expense, submit the normal paperwork for reimbursement. If the employer dances around the outside of propriety, so will his employees.
2. The company must have an open-door policy of some kind. If the owner cannot commit the time necessary, then he must assign a manager to do it— and in return keep his own door open to that manager. Although every employee is certainly entitled to his privacy, some of those private happenings will directly affect your business, and you must be aware of them.
3. Establish some kind of rehabilitation program for your employees who develop

addictions. Addictions are one of the biggest causes of white-collar crime. Addictions to drugs, alcohol, gambling, and even computing have cost companies millions. Letting someone go because he has an addiction is being looked upon these days as a type of discrimination, and, frankly, it does nothing to solve the problem. The person will simply find a job elsewhere and continue with his cycle of misbehavior.

4. Provide proper work tools for your employees so that they do not have to improvise. Looking for ways to "make do" open doors that you really don't want opened. I once worked for a fellow who decided to computerize his business. He spent many thousands of dollars on a nice computer, but the only software he was willing to invest in was word processing. When I told him I had to have something for accounting, I was told he had spent enough on the computer, and I had all I needed. That poor man actually believed that he was fully computerized, and I could not convince him otherwise. There is a misconception among computer illiterates that if something is printed on a dot matrix, it is totally accurate. I finally started printing out the financial statements through word processing, and he was perfectly happy "knowing" that the computer was watching things for him.

5. Pay your help fairly. You may save a dollar an hour in salary for your bookkeeper—a grand total of some $2,000 a year—but just think what it could cost you if that bookkeeper feels abused because of the unfair wages.

6. Check into the possibilities offered by pre-employment honesty testing programs. If you are responsible for hiring new employees, these programs can save you a lot of work and a lot of grief. Pre-employment honesty testing has come a long way in the past five years. It no longer involves sending your prospective employee to another firm for testing. You can do it in-house, as part of your basic interview. It is now possible to mail-order software that does most of your evaluations for you. For a nominal price, you will receive a diskette that prints out the questionnaire for your applicant to complete. This questionnaire is worded very carefully to measure the responses and make computer evaluation quick and accurate.

CONCLUSION

Although some of Roger Self's and Donna Beitel's opinions may differ from ours, the thrusts of their views are similar. Both of them realize that owners and managers are, to a large extent, responsible for the actions of their employees—including stealing. If they share responsibility for their actions, then they also are capable of influencing them. Donna's point about not being paid properly and not even being recognized for her work is good. As consultants to business for more than a decade, we can tell you without hesitation that most employees feel that way. They are underpaid and unrecognized.

Employee theft is a huge problem, but it can be reduced significantly. The strategies for dealing with employee theft presented in this book work. We urge you to consider them carefully. For your information, we have included as Appendix 2 a checklist on how to prevent employee theft that was prepared by the Crime Prevention Manual Task Force in Virginia. It provides some interesting suggestions for you to consider.

CHAPTER 4

A Strategy for Reducing Employee Theft

As stated previously, employee theft is one of the most serious problems facing U.S. businesses and costs at least $40 billion annually.[1] To put the problem into perspective, $40 billion is about 1.5 percent of the value of all world trade.[2] Other estimates suggest that employee theft may cost employers as much as $120 billion annually.

Estimates also suggest that employees steal billions of dollars (maybe as much as $200 billion) annually by cheating on time cards and expense accounts,[3] and the problem is escalating rapidly. A study by John Clark and Richard Hollinger found that about one-third of a typical company's employees will admit to some form of stealing.[4] Others have suggested that one in ten employees is a bona fide thief, and these people will steal from you whenever they have the opportunity. Another one in ten employees will never steal from you, no matter what the circumstances. That leaves eight in ten employees, the vast majority, who consider themselves honest, but who can be led to take things from you if they think everyone else is doing it too. These are normal, well-adjusted, honest people who believe that it is appropriate for them to take things if their peers are doing it. This is not a new or novel view. What parent has not had to explain to his or her children that they must do what is right even though all of their friends are doing wrong. "You cannot just follow the leader," we say, "because that approach will inevitably lead to trouble."

To understand how your employees arrive at the conclusion that they can take things from you and that it is not stealing, it is essential to look at the situation from their perspective. They think that they are reasonably intelligent people and that you are at least as smart as they are.

They know that their fellow employees are taking things and doing little, if anything, to conceal it. From the typical employee's point of view, if they know what is going on, then you must know it too. They assume you know about it, and because you are doing nothing to prevent it, then it must be all right. Therefore, it makes perfect sense to the vast majority of your employees to take things, and they would be offended if you suggested that they were stealing.

What triggered the rapid rise in employee theft? Some experts believe that the decline of the work ethic in the United States and the rise of the welfare state in the last half of this century are to blame. Others think that it resulted from the disillusionment and cynicism that plagued the United States after Vietnam and Watergate.[5] Others have proposed that the increase in employee theft comes on the heels of two related phenomena: the decline in the importance of moral values and an increase in the permissiveness of the people in our society. One author said that the problem is a product of the "me" generation's appetite for instant gratification.[6] Others suggest that the problem may be the result of poor management practices in most U.S. businesses. Personal problems that might trigger employee theft include greed, excessive personal debt, gambling, extramarital relations, and drug and/or alcohol abuse.

A DIFFICULT PROBLEM TO SOLVE

Employee theft is a difficult problem to solve for many reasons. Probably the most important reason is that there is no simple, straightforward definition of what constitutes employee theft. Businesses in the United States represent a wide range of values and beliefs. Their owners and managers see the world differently, and they define theft differently. Therefore, every organization must define theft for its own particular needs and circumstances. Most owners and managers, however, naively assume that all employees know what theft is, and that the employees all see things as they do. This simply is not true. Thus a critical first step in developing an effective theft reduction strategy is to actually define what theft is.

The process used to define theft should be participatory; that is, employees should be as involved in it as possible. In large firms it is not necessary for every employee to be involved in the process, but a fair representation of them should be. In smaller firms it would be a good idea to include as many employees in the process as possible. The rationale for including employees in the process is simple. The more involved they are, the more committed they should be to the decisions made and the more likely they and their fellow employees will not steal from the company. As a first step in the process, a committee usually is formed and charged with the responsibility to develop a statement that will clarify for everyone what will, and what will not, be accepted. If they do their job well, they will establish the foundation for the other parts of the theft reduction strategy.

Equity in the workplace is another issue. If people believe that they are not being rewarded properly for their work, sometimes they try to get what they believe they deserve by stealing. In their eyes, however, they are not stealing. They are just getting what they believe belongs to them anyway. Donna Beitel talked about how she felt when she got very little money and almost no recognition from her employer when her work resulted in a 600 percent increase in earnings from a portfolio under her control. It definitely contributed to her stealing, although it did not cause her to steal. There is no good excuse for employees to steal; there also is no good excuse for owners and managers to be insensitive to the financial and ego needs of their employees. This insensitivity can be expensive for both parties, that is, the employee and the employer.

Other employees retaliate against management by stealing. In their opinions, they are not stealing either; they are simply getting even with their bosses. It is impossible to do the job of an owner or manager and not make some of your employees mad, very mad, at you once in a while. But some owners and managers behave as if they do not care what their employees think about anything they might do. When employees believe that owners and managers do not care, it makes them angry, and it increases the likelihood that they will steal from the company. Therefore, it is good business not to alienate and anger your employees any more than you must.

But it would be foolish not to recognize that some people are virtually bankrupt when it comes to morals and values, and they are simply thieves. They will steal no matter what, and they do not even attempt to justify their behavior. It is difficult to understand with certainty why legitimate thieves steal. Some people blame the public schools for not teaching morals and values. Others blame parents for not raising their children correctly. Still others say that people are born with predispositions, and some of them are born with whatever it is that makes them steal. Although we cannot explain with absolute certainty why thieves steal, we can say with absolute certainty that you must get them out of your business, or they can bankrupt it.

The purpose of this chapter is to examine the critical factors that must be addressed in the development of a successful theft reduction strategy. Both strategic and operational factors must be considered. Strategic factors have to do with the formulation, implementation, and evaluation of the firm's strategy, whereas operational factors are more tactical in nature. Exhibit 4.1 presents an Employee Theft Reduction Model that takes these factors into account.

Exhibit 4.1
Employee Theft Reduction Model

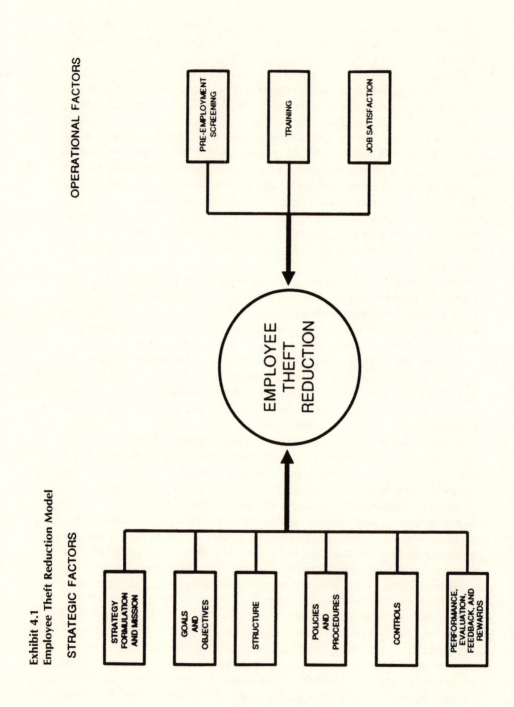

OPERATIONAL FACTORS

STRATEGIC FACTORS

PRE-EMPLOYMENT SCREENING

TRAINING

JOB SATISFACTION

EMPLOYEE THEFT REDUCTION

STRATEGY FORMULATION AND MISSION

GOALS AND OBJECTIVES

STRUCTURE

POLICIES AND PROCEDURES

CONTROLS

PERFORMANCE, EVALUATION, FEEDBACK, AND REWARDS

STRATEGIC FACTORS

Strategy Formulation and the Mission Statement

Strategy Formulation. The process used to formulate strategy affects the climate in an organization and the incidence of employee theft. Employee involvement in the process, to the extent that it can be accommodated, is good business for at least two reasons. First, the more input they provide as the firm's strategy is being developed, the more the strategy will reflect their values and beliefs. In addition, their involvement in the process helps to refine their views and clarify their beliefs. Thus it is easier for them to live with the final result. Second, the more involved they are in the process, the more committed they should be to making the strategy work effectively.

The Mission Statement. A mission statement identifies a firm's long-term commitments and directions; it serves as a decision guide for all employees, and should address the basic philosophical issues that are critical to the firm's success. A recent study revealed that a significant relation exists between a firm's performance and the inclusion of this kind of information in the mission statement.[7] Thus the specific values and beliefs that define a firm's philosophy should be addressed in the mission statement in detail, and it should be distributed to all employees.

Values and Beliefs. Two values that are fundamental to any successful theft reduction strategy are honesty and integrity in every situation, and both of these values should be addressed in the mission statement. Managers must stress that honesty and integrity are important, and that everyone in the firm is expected to make decisions that reflect these principles. Additionally, everyone must understand that dishonesty will not be tolerated.

Quality work and respect for co-workers are two other values that affect employee attitudes toward theft, and they also should be addressed in a mission statement. If a firm stresses quality and attention to detail, the jobs in the firm will become more meaningful to employees, and they will tend to develop a sense of pride in their work and in themselves that will inevitably influence their attitudes toward theft. Similarly, respect for co-workers influences attitudes toward theft. By promoting respect for others, employees will develop better attitudes in general and better attitudes toward other people's property in particular.

Instilling and Reinforcing Values. The owners and managers of a firm must communicate their values and beliefs to their employees consistently and frequently to reinforce their importance. If this is not done, employees may never embrace the company's philosophy. In addition, they must set examples of honesty and integrity for all employees to see and follow. Otherwise, the employees will inevitably become disenchanted. If the owners and managers of the business fail to live by the corporate creed, they cannot expect their employees to live by it either. As Thomas R. Horton, president and chief executive officer of the American Management Association, put it, "progress in a company's fight against crime can begin only when managers at all levels regard themselves as ethical role models—avoiding conflicts of interest, clarifying the kind of business conduct expected by the company and taking seriously the fact that we must be like Caesar's wife—beyond suspicion."[8]

Owners and managers cannot assume that identifying and communicating the correct values alone will ensure loyalty and prevent theft. Other methods to reduce employee theft also must be considered.

Goals and Objectives

The level of employee theft also is affected by the goals and objectives the firm is seeking to achieve and the process it uses to develop them. For example, an ambitious strategy emphasizing high growth may put the employees under such extreme pressure that they behave dishonestly to satisfy the expectations of their superiors. When this happens, a culture more tolerant of dishonesty in general and of theft in particular develops.

Additionally, goals that are too ambitious may tax the company's information system and its ability to monitor the quality and quantity of performance adequately. If this happens, it could lead to inadequate reporting of operating results and could weaken the firm's formal and informal communication systems, both of which are extremely important in an effective theft reduction strategy.

It should be pointed out that we are not arguing against rapid growth. We are suggesting, however, that the formulation of challenging, fair, and achievable goals is critical to a firm's success. A mission statement proclaiming a company's concern about honesty and integrity will become meaningless in an atmosphere in which short-term performance is prized above all else. Such inconsistencies lead to confusion and cynicism among employees and ultimately increase employee theft.

Structure

The way a business organizes and structures its operation also affects employee theft. The establishment of divisions and/or departments segregates responsibilities so that a system of checks and balances can be used to reduce the likelihood of a thief going undetected. At the same time it creates opportunities for enhanced cooperation and participation by employees, teamwork, and coordination between divisions and/or departments. The additional benefits of employees working together to solve problems and accomplish objectives include a greater sense of belonging, increased loyalty and motivation, and values that are more consistently applied and monitored. Each of these attributes of effective organizational structure helps to reduce employee theft.

When designing or redesigning a firm's structure, careful attention should be given to span of control issues. It currently is in vogue to expand managers' spans of control to the point where they cannot interfere too much in the details of their subordinates' work and to reduce the number of levels of management. There is merit in this approach because it forces managers to manage and keeps them from duplicating the work of their employees. Managers whose spans of control are too broad, however, have less time to devote to team-building and the promotion of company values, two critical management responsibilities. When carried too far, this approach may have negative effects on loyalty, morale, and productivity. It also could have the long-term effect of increasing employee theft.

Policies and Procedures

Establishing and implementing appropriate policies, procedures, and rules is one of the most important links in the theft reduction chain. Their creation helps to clarify what theft is in a given firm, to establish acceptable limits on employee behavior, to provide consistent standards for dealing with problems that arise, and to communicate management's intentions to employees at all levels in the organization. It must be clear to everyone that theft is unacceptable and that it will not be tolerated. Every employee should understand that dismissal and prosecution are the penalties for stealing from the firm. In a community so dependent on trust and cooperation, there is no good alternative to this approach.

Addressing employee theft directly in a company's policies, procedures, and rules is extremely important. The formation of an antitheft policy is one of the factors Clark and Hollinger found to be related to the reduction of employee theft.[9] Although excessive use of an antitheft policy may have a negative effect on productivity, creativity, and morale, consistent application of established policies and procedures is essential.

Furthermore, it is important to communicate policies, procedures, and rules in written and oral forms. Forms of written distribution include paycheck inserts, company newsletter articles, interoffice memos, and notices on bulletin boards. By ensuring frequent communication, management will avoid the "I didn't know" response when confronting an employee who has violated company policy.

Controls

The physical and accounting controls implemented by an organization are of paramount importance to the reduction of employee theft. Adequate controls serve to prevent, detect, and report incidents of theft, and they may be tailored to the specific needs of an organization. Basic controls form a primary barrier against the problem; their absence paves the way for increased employee theft.

Physical controls serve the primary purpose of protecting a company's assets. Through the implementation of mechanisms such as security guards, locked doors, and identification cards, an employee's access to company assets is restricted and the incidence of theft is reduced.

Common accounting controls, such as segregation of duties, also constrain an employee's behavior and limit his access to company assets. Additionally, they provide accountability for actions and develop an environment in which there is less opportunity to steal. An effective accounting system also records and communicates operational results that may indicate vulnerable areas before problems escalate to crisis proportions.

Although internal controls are necessary in every organization, the dependence on controls should not be so excessive that they reduce employee productivity and morale. Loose controls in a firm without strong values and belief against stealing will result in increased employee theft. On the other hand, tight controls in a company with strong and well-established values against stealing will be viewed as excessive and could result in decreased productivity.[10] Finding the appropriate level of internal control, therefore, is a critical management job that requires good judgment.

Performance Evaluation, Feedback, and Rewards

Performance Evaluation. Performance evaluation, feedback, and rewards are all essential in an effective theft reduction strategy. The evaluation process should begin with an assessment of a person's performance in light of established goals and objectives. In many instances performance evaluations focus almost entirely on "what was accomplished," and almost no attention is given to "how it was accomplished." Implementation of an effective theft reduction strategy requires that employees understand that the latter is important and that honesty and integrity will be rewarded. By the same token, they must understand that dishonesty will not be tolerated.

Feedback. When evaluation results are communicated to employees in regular feedback sessions, they know if their performance is on target and how to improve if their performance is not up to par. Feedback sessions should be held frequently, and they should be used to coach and counsel employees. Furthermore, feedback sessions provide a wonderful opportunity for owners and managers to reinforce the values and beliefs that are essential for the success of the firm and to focus on the whole range of a person's accomplishments. Managers should avoid the temptation to use feedback sessions simply to let people know where they went wrong.

Rewards. Providing feedback about performance is important, but rewarding successful performance is essential. If employees are told that honesty and integrity count, then they should be rewarded for maintaining high standards. "By recognizing the contributions of employees to the success of the business in tangible and intangible ways, management can increase morale, reduce negative feelings that affect how employees perceive their company, and reduce the likelihood that employee theft will occur."[11]

Designing an appropriate reward system also helps to reduce employee theft and promote desired behavior. Many systems, however, reward one form of behavior while hoping for another. For example, "the organization that asks employees to set challenging, risky goals, only to face smaller paychecks and possibly damaged careers if these goals are not accomplished, breeds resentment and a lack of trust in its employees."[12] Such negative sentiments are likely to result in deviant behavior, including theft.

Profit-sharing plans have been used effectively to reduce the incidence of employee theft. At J. C. Penney, for example, employees are told that they have a stake in the theft problem because every dollar that is stolen is a dollar that will not be used in the company's profit-sharing plan. "If the company experiences losses, everybody loses."[13] Loss prevention programs also may be used to enlist employee assistance in reducing theft. For example, some firms have identified an acceptable level of inventory shrinkage. When shrinkage drops below that level, half of the savings are placed in a fund that is distributed to employees.[14]

OPERATIONAL FACTORS

Pre-employment Screening

Probably the most critical role of pre-employment screening is to identify people who are likely to conform to organizational expectations. The people doing the screening should know what the company expects from its employees in terms of performance, congeniality, professional demeanor, and so on. But they also should know what values and beliefs employees must possess to succeed with the firm. Values and beliefs are formed early in life, and they cannot easily be changed. If the values and beliefs that lead to success in the firm are not shared by the employees, they will not be happy and probably will not be productive. Also, if potential employees are dishonest, it is unlikely that the company can alter their behavior quickly or significantly. Thus recruiters should not pursue potential employees about whom they harbor significant doubts.

As established previously, it is much easier and less expensive to prevent potential thieves from joining an organization than it is to apprehend criminals once they are hired. Pre-employment screening is used to weed out bad applicants and to investigate borderline cases.[15] Consistent application of appropriate screening techniques has the additional advantage of discouraging people with histories of theft from even applying for a job with the company.[16]

Personal Interviews. We have already indicated that the personal interview is an important step in the pre-employment screening process. Personal interaction with an applicant provides valuable insights into his or her character, potential for theft, and susceptibility to influence from dishonest co-workers that cannot be obtained in any other way. As stated previously, however, relying exclusively on personal interviews with applicants is unwise. Gifted thieves have developed great skill in masking their true identities.

Checking References. A variety of other methods can be utilized, depending on the size of the firm and the amount of money it is willing to spend on this process. A relatively easy procedure is to ask for personal references and to carefully check them. Again, although they are easy to obtain, personal references do not always provide the objective information employers need. Friends can lie for their friends, and past employers often are unwilling to share negative information about former employees for fear that their reputations will be tarnished or that lawsuits might ensue. Thus one should always exercise caution when interpreting information obtained from a personal reference provided by a potential employee.

Obtaining Credit Reports. Another simple and inexpensive prescreening procedure we have mentioned previously is to obtain a credit report on each applicant. There are two schools of thought on this approach. The first holds that if a person does not pay his debts promptly, or if he has a history of not repaying all the money he owes, then he is probably a poor money manager and, thus, a bad employment risk. On the other hand, as we already have established, some experts argue that a good credit record is no guarantee that a person is not a thief. An applicant may be stealing from others to pay his debts.[17] Nevertheless, at the very least, credit reports will provide information on potential employees' repayment habits, and they will allow evaluators to make more informed judgments about inconsistencies between their life-styles and incomes.

Psychological Testing. The last pre-employment screening method is psychological testing. Though this testing can be more expensive than paper-and-pencil honesty tests, it often provides valuable and accurate information about an applicant's personality and attitudes toward theft. Unlike polygraph tests, which are now illegal for use in most pre-employment screening situations, written tests do not infer guilt or wrongdoing, but they measure what an applicant might be likely to do under certain circumstances.

To reiterate, if an owner or manager has doubts about a person's honesty, an employment offer should not be made. As previously indicated, estimates suggest that 10 percent of potential employees will always steal; 10 percent will never steal; and the remaining 80 percent are honest but can be tempted to steal if placed in the right setting.[18] If a thief is hired and he steals from the business, his presence will inevitably influence the 80 percent of employees who otherwise would never think of violating antitheft norms.[19]

Training

Training and development programs also influence the likelihood of employee theft. They provide employees with opportunities to expand their horizons, to increase their earning potential, and to move into more responsible positions. In addition, effective training programs give employees a sense of control over their destinies that many of them will not experience unless owners and managers take the initiative in this matter. An employee who is able to recognize opportunities within the firm and who knows that he can take advantage of them if he is willing to work hard will be more productive and loyal. Loyalty, ultimately, has the effect of reducing employee theft.

Employee training programs also provide owners and managers with opportunities to reinforce the firm's values and beliefs and to explain the logic behind its policies and procedures. Among all the procedures used by retailers to control losses, employee training programs are the method used most often. A study conducted by Arthur Young found that 83 percent of retailers do some sort of antitheft training. When asked to assess the effectiveness of their programs, 92 percent of the respondents rated the programs as very effective or somewhat effective.[20]

Job Satisfaction

The importance of creating a healthy organizational climate, one that promotes job satisfaction and fosters honesty and integrity, must not be underestimated in the fight against employee theft. In their research, Hollinger and Clark conclude that job dissatisfaction is a fundamental reason for employee theft. Their findings suggest that "all age groups of employees who are dissatisfied with the quality of their present employment experience are significantly more likely to seek unauthorized redress for these perceived inequities from the organization via its tangible property or expected levels of productivity."[21]

Two-Way Communication. We have emphasized that two-way communication also plays an important role in creating a healthy work environment. "Giving employees an opportunity to discuss their problems and acknowledging they merit consideration provides positive reinforcement for employees and makes them feel more a part of the company."[22] Surveys, informal meetings, and even gripe sessions provide employees with opportunities to voice their opinions and/or vent their frustrations. These and other forms of communication also enable employees to address their grievances and discuss their attitudes in a constructive way. Additionally, they provide management with extremely important information about existing and potential problems. We have included as Appendix 3 a paper by Kenneth Kovach titled "What Motivates Employees? Workers and Supervisors Give Different Answers." It suggests that employers and employees do not communicate very well, and we think it is worthwhile reading.

Proper Treatment of Employees. Research indicates that treating employees with dignity, respect, and trust has a significant effect on employee theft.[23] Hollinger and Clark found that "employees who felt that their employers and supervisors were concerned genuinely with their workers' best interest reported the least theft and deviance. When employees felt exploited by the company or by their supervisors, [Hollinger and Clark] were not surprised to find these workers more involved in acts against the organization as a mechanism to correct perceptions of inequity or injustice."[24] As established in the opening chapter, "it's more difficult to steal from a friend than from someone who doesn't care about you."[25]

Job Enrichment. Hollinger and Clark concluded that factors intrinsic to the work environment are central to explaining why employees steal from their employers. Indeed, the significance of intrinsic factors was confirmed by Kenneth Kovach's research, which indicates that employees consider "interesting work" to be the most important job characteristic.[26] Management must pay particular attention to job factors that influence employee attitudes, such as the work itself, the opportunity for achievement and advancement, and recognition for work done. Job enrichment programs are designed to focus the attention of owners, managers, and employees on these factors. In addition, "providing employees with challenging and interesting tasks gives them less time to concentrate on stealing and is important for those with high growth need and achievement motivation levels."[27]

SUMMARY AND CONCLUSION

Two sets of factors influence the level of employee theft in an organization: strategic and operational. The strategic factors include strategy formulation and mission, goals and objectives, structure, policies and procedures, controls, and performance evaluation, feedback, and rewards. The operational factors include pre-employment screening, training, and job satisfaction.

Developing an effective theft reduction strategy in an organization begins with an awareness by owners and managers that the identification of questions and issues related to employee theft in each of these areas is critical. Owners and managers ultimately must take the initiative to create a work environment in their firms that is conducive to high levels of honesty, integrity, morale, loyalty, and productivity, and low levels of employee theft.

NOTES

1. Harry Bacas, "To Stop a Thief," *Nation's Business*, 75 (June 1987), pp. 16–23.

2. Roy Carter, "Employee Theft Often Appears Legitimate," *Accountancy*, 100 (July 1987); pp. 75–77.

3. Rod Willis, "White-Collar Crime: The Threat from Within," *Management Review*, 75 (January 1986), pp. 22–32.

4. John Clark and Richard Hollinger, *Theft by Employees in Work Organizations* (Lexington, Mass.: Lexington Books, 1983).

5. James Walls, "Preventing Employee Theft," *Management Review*, 74 (September 1985), pp. 48–50.

6. Ron Zemke, "Employee Theft: How to Cut Your Losses," *Training*, 23 (May 1986), pp. 74–78.

7. John Pearce and Fred David, "Corporate Mission Statements: The Bottom Line," *Academy of Management Executive*, May 1987, pp. 109–15.

8. Bacas, "To Stop a Thief."

9. Clark and Hollinger, *Theft by Employees*.

10. Neil H. Snyder and Karen Blair, "Dealing with Employee Theft," *Business Horizons*, May-June 1989, pp. 1–8.

11. Ibid.

12. Steven Kerr, "On the Folly of Rewarding A, While Hoping for B," *Academy of Management Journal*, 18 (December 1975), pp. 769–83.

13. Zemke, "Employee Theft."

14. Ibid.

15. Daniel E. Sosnowski, "Curbing Employee Theft—How Firms Do It," *Security Management*, 29 (September 1985), pp. 109–12.

16. Clark and Hollinger, *Theft by Employees*.

17. Walls, "Preventing Employee Theft."

18. Kurt G. Leuse, "Security Programs: Only as Good as We Make Them," *The Office*, 100 (August 1984), pp. 91–92, 100.

19. Clark and Hollinger, *Theft by Employees*.

20. Zemke, "Employee Theft."

21. Clark and Hollinger, *Theft by Employees* .

22. Snyder and Blair, "Dealing with Employee Theft."

23. Robert R. Taylor, "Your Role in the Prevention of Employee Theft," *Management Solutions*, 31 (August 1986), pp. 20–25.

24. Clark and Hollinger, *Theft by Employees*.

25. Taylor, "Prevention of Employee Theft."

26. Kenneth A. Kovack, "What Motivates Employees? Workers and Supervisors Give Different Answers," *Business Horizons*, 30 (September-October 1987), pp. 58–65.

27. Taylor, "Prevention of Employee Theft."

CHAPTER 5

Ethics and Employee Theft

It is obvious by now that employee theft is a pervasive problem. *Time* speaks of a "light-fingered work ethic."[1] James Walls, in *Vital Speeches of the Day*, calls the workplace "America's hot bed of crime."[2] Robert Cameron, in *Venture* magazine, says, "You come to the point where you just cross your fingers and hope they won't rob you blind."[3] The "they" to whom he refers are employees, and the "hot bed of crime" is your business.

THE CONCEPT OF EMPLOYEE THEFT

Employee theft may be tangible, as in the case of an employee taking inventory, supplies, or cash moneys from a firm; less tangible, as in the case of an employee falsifying records or expense reports for personal benefit when such benefit has not been earned; or intangible, as in the case of time theft or demotivating colleagues, thereby reducing their effectiveness to the firm.

Whether tangible or intangible, employee theft occurs when an employee takes from the firm something to which he or she is not entitled and that, if known to the firm, would not be granted to the employee. At one extreme is an employee taking a 50-cent box of paper clips for personal use to another extreme of an employee who takes machinery valued at $50,000. Although the profit consequences of the former are not as severe as the latter, both acts of theft have moral consequences to the firm and to the employee, and each will change both the firm and the employee.

ETHICS AND THEFT

To understand the moral consequences of employee theft, an examination of the concept of ethics is a starting point. Ethics have been defined as "a systematic attempt, through the use of reason, to make sense of our individual and social moral experience, in such a way as to determine the rules that ought to govern human conduct and the values worth pursuing in life."[4]

Ethics are concerned with evaluating actions and decisions from the perspective of moral principles and values. In its simplest meaning, being ethical is doing the right thing rather than the wrong thing. It is being moral, honest, correct, and fair in everything a person undertakes. It is living with a set of values and principles that guide the decisions and actions of a person. Such values and principles include the following:

- Obey the law
- Do not harm others
- Respect the rights and property of others
- Never lie, cheat, or steal
- Keep promises and contracts
- Be fair to all people
- Help those in need
- Encourage and reinforce these values and principles in others

These values and principles, at the simplest level of ethics, have been called "moral common sense."[5] When applied to the situation of employee theft, the concept of ethics at the level of moral common sense would suggest that employees should not steal. Such is a principle that is valued. A person, both in personal life and in employment life, should not steal, and when faced with the potential of theft, an ethical person, using moral common sense, does the right thing rather than the wrong thing and does not steal.

But employees do steal, and employee theft is a real problem, noted earlier in this book to be valued at more than $40 billion a year and to be increasing at a 15 percent annual rate. The notion of moral common sense does not stand in the face of the magnitude of employee theft. Moral common sense is a simple, straightforward notion. Its simplicity, however, which would have sufficed at an earlier age, does not hold today. Employee theft is a major problem, a problem not prevented or resolved by applying moral common sense, a problem exacerbated by rationalization, and perhaps better understood by lifting the analysis from the fundamental level of moral common sense to the more complex levels of ethical relativism, rules (deontology), and consequences (teleology).

THE CONCEPT OF ETHICAL RELATIVISM

Rationalization

A justification used by some employees to rationalize their act of theft is that others are doing it too. This is the "when in Rome, do as the Romans do" rationalization. Because the employee perceives that other employees are partaking in theft, he or she rationalizes that the act is appropriate. That is, he or she develops the belief that it is morally acceptable to steal from the employer because everyone else is perceived to be stealing as well.

Added to the "everyone is doing it" rationalization are other reasons to justify the act. Examples of some of the reasons employees give for stealing are as follows:

- They are not fairly compensated
- Items taken are of small value (e.g., small parts, office supplies, food stuffs, and the like) and will not be missed by the employer
- The employer expects (i.e., approves) that employees will steal or participate in shrinking the inventory and has arranged insurance coverage to offset the loss
- They will not be caught in the theft and, if detected, will be lightly punished, if at all, by the firm
- The company has engaged in unfair labor practices or is planning a reduction in force; hence they should take (i.e., steal) whatever is available as a form of compensation
- The company is bad or in some other way evil and needs to be justifiably punished by the employee through theft
- The company is big and impersonal, and the employee is hardly known; therefore, stealing is justified to strike back at the big, impersonal entity

These reasons become part of a person's system of belief—a system of belief that is assumed by the person to be widely held, logical, and axiomatic—a system of belief used to justify the act of theft.

Ethical Relativism

In justifying the act of theft on the basis that "everyone is doing it," the employee is applying ethical relativism as the logic in use. The concept of ethical relativism is anchored in the notion that "people in different cultures, as well as people within a given culture, hold divergent moral views on particular issues."[6] For example, in the United States it is morally unacceptable to engage in bribery, but in another country it may be morally acceptable and a common business practice. An example within the United States is the divergent views on the issue of capital punishment. People on each side of the issue have reasons to justify or condemn the practice and are able to articulate reasons in ways they perceive to be logical.

The concept of ethical relativism gives explanation as to why, within a single firm, there may be employed people who hold divergent views on theft. For instance, some employees' system of belief or logic leads them to morally accept stealing from the firm. On the other hand, some employees have moral standards such that, no matter how they view the firm or how it has treated them, to steal from the firm is wrong and is never considered.

Although the concept of ethical relativism gives explanation as to why, within a single firm, some employees may steal while others do not, the concept does not justify employee theft. Rather, as in most cultures, it may be argued that stealing in our culture is morally unacceptable. Said another way, people in a variety of cultures, including ours, hold the view that theft is morally unacceptable or wrong. Given that theft as a concept is wrong, employee theft also is morally unacceptable and wrong.

RULES AND CONSEQUENCES

The basic argument that employee theft is morally unacceptable and wrong has been framed at the level of moral common sense. The ethical analysis, however, must rise to a higher level to fully explore the concept of employee theft from the viewpoint of ethics and to present ethical theories useful in both understanding and preventing employee theft. Specifically, the higher level of analysis considers rules (deontological theory) and consequences (teleological theory).

Rules

Deontological theory is concerned with the rules used in making a decision or taking an action—in other words, the rules that might be used by a person when deciding whether or not to participate in employee theft. Here, two rules are considered: the categorical imperative and the golden rule.

- The categorical imperative requires that people never take actions that they would not recommend to others.[7] That is, people should not take an action (e.g., participate in employee theft) unless they believe that it could be recommended to others. In short, would the person be able to stand at the next company meeting, admit employee theft, and recommend it to others? If the answer is no, the action fails the categorical imperative and probably is not ethical. Not being able to tell others is "a clarion call that what is planned or has been done may not be ethical. The categorical imperative, is one of the best and simplest tests of ethics and should, perhaps, be the first test of ethics to be employed when in doubt about a particular action or decision."[8]

- The golden rule—do unto others as you would have them do unto you—advises people to act in the way they would want others to act toward them. Employees considering theft should ask, under the test of the golden rule, whether they would want the firm to steal from them. If the answer is no, then, under the golden rule, employee theft is not justified.

In each of the deontological theories, the categorical imperative and the golden rule, the person is faced with a *yes* or *no* alternative. If the answer to the ethical question posed by these theories is no, then the action is not ethical and is one in which the employee should not participate. The practice of employee theft fails both the categorical imperative and the golden rule. But what of the consequences of employee theft? Might there be consequences that justify the practice?

Consequences

Telelogical theory is concerned with the consequences of an action or decision. Here two concepts are considered—the utilitarian principle and egoism.

- The utilitarian principle asks that an individual act in a way to produce the greatest good for the greatest number.[9] Employee theft produces ill-gotten gain for the individual, but does not produce good for the greatest number. An employee seeking to do an act for the greatest number would do something to benefit the company, its customers, and its community. Employee theft does not benefit the company (i.e., the greater entity) and only benefits the individual in the form of profit from the ill-gotten gain. Here again, an employee, when contemplating a theft, is faced with a yes or no situation under the utilitarian principle. Will the act produce the greatest good for the greatest number? If the answer is no, the act fails the utilitarian principle and, most likely, is not ethical.

- The concept of egoism is about self-interest. It is divided into psychological egoism—that individuals do act to benefit themselves—and ethical egoism—that individuals ought to act to benefit themselves.[10] Some would argue that we are a very egoist society, a society in which individuals put themselves first in all that they do. In the situation of employee theft, individuals are egoists, in that they perceive the act of theft to be in their best interest, no matter how ill-gotten the gain or the hurt to another person. An egoist "does not care about the welfare of others except insofar as it affects her or his own welfare."[11] This explanation fits a thief, a person who, by the very act of theft, demonstrates a lack of care and respect for others.

THE ETHICAL PERSPECTIVE

The consequences of doing good to others (utilitarianism) and self-interest (egoism) give insight to employee theft. A person who has concern for and wants to do good for others (utilitarianism) may be less likely to steal from an employer than a person who is egotistical in orientation. Likewise, people who care about what others would think of them if the theft be known (categorical imperative) and who act in a way they would want to be treated by others (golden rule) are, again, less likely to steal than a person who does not have these concerns. These thoughts, taken together with the earlier discussion of moral common sense, give understanding of employee theft from an ethical perspective.

An application of the ethical perspective in employee theft is found in the written honesty tests reported to be in use in more than 5,000 companies nationwide.[12] These tests, which were administered to 3.5 million job applicants in 1988, cost $5 to $15 each and may be used on a pre-employment or after employment basis.[13] Designed from the ethical theories presented above, the tests attempt to measure a person's ethics and morality. Although no single answer in the tests indicates a thief, those who administer and score the tests look for patterns in the answers. Series of questions measure whether the person has concern for others, his or her disposition to honesty in both small- and large-value situations, and his or her logic-in-use, or how he or she reasons through an ethical situation. Scores are determined for each person and placed within a range to indicate whether he or she is more likely to be honest or to be dishonest.

Honesty tests are an application of ethics in dealing with the problem of employee theft. The tests are based on ethical theory and, by posing a series of ethical situations, attempt to measure a person's tendency toward honesty. Ryan A. Kuhn, president of Reid Psychological Systems in Chicago, has done a great deal of research on the psychology of theft, and his company is probably the industry leader in the honesty-test field. His research findings are useful in helping us understand more about the typical thief. For example, he has learned that people who steal believe that others do it frequently, fantasize about committing the act frequently, and do not believe that thieves should be disciplined for their acts. He also says that dishonest people typically bring other problems with them into the workplace. They are far more likely to demonstrate pathological psychological profiles, to abuse drugs, to quit or be fired, to experience hostile encounters, and to file bogus insurance and worker's compensation claims. The *Reid Report*, the original pencil-and-paper honesty test that typically reduces theft incidences and turnover by about 50 percent, costs between $7 and $15 to use—a small price to pay for extremely valuable information.

THE EMPLOYER IN EMPLOYEE THEFT

Thus far, the focus has been on the employee. Of equal importance in an ethical analysis of employee theft is the employer and the ethical obligations of the employer. These include honesty, prevention, fairness, and instilling ethics in the organization.

Management Honesty

We have previously established that management honesty is of paramount importance. In a study that examined management honesty as a factor in preventing employee theft, the conclusion was that "if employees think top management is behaving honestly, they will probably think they are expected to behave honestly. But if employees perceive that top management is dishonest, they will be more inclined to justify and excuse their own dishonesty."[14]

Thus dishonesty in management will, in time, induce employee dishonesty. Through the actions of management, employees will be moved or conditioned toward honesty or dishonesty. It is imperative that management set an example. If managers participate in such things as insider trading, price fixing, check kiting, expense padding, time and material theft, and other acts of white-collar crime, there is a danger that these dishonest actions of management eventually will induce employees toward dishonesty. Management dishonesty, ultimately, will be manifest as employee theft. Therefore, to prevent employees from stealing based on the perception of a dishonest management, leaders in the organization must maintain the highest levels of honesty.

Management Prevention

Management is morally obliged to recognize their responsibility to their employees in preventing the opportunities for employee theft. Managers should "spot the temptations that might induce employees to steal and isolate these temptations so they can be eliminated."[15] As stated before, eliminating temptation can be done by establishing internal controls and security systems within the organization. These controls include inventory systems, security systems, financial controls, employment-screening systems, and the like. Management must be concerned with prevention—this is the second moral obligation of management.

Management Fairness

Management also has an obligation to be concerned about employee theft and to make that concern known in the organization. If management is perceived as not caring about the problem, does not have a clear policy on employee theft, and does not enforce that policy or applies it more leniently to managers, the spirit of fairness necessary to deter employee theft will be eroded. Management must be concerned about employee theft and treat all employees similarly when dealing with the problem.

Management-Instilled Ethics

Management has a moral obligation to instill ethics in the organization. This means that management must nurture ethics in the company and create an open environment for discussion of ethics. A code of ethics should be in place in every company; it should be widely promulgated and discussed with each employee. Meetings and seminars on ethics should be regularly conducted, and ethics and employee theft should be a point of discussion in an employee's annual review with management. Procedures for bringing questions of ethics or of employee theft to management should be established. And violators of the code of ethics should be treated fairly and swiftly. In essence, management must lead by example.

CONCLUSION

Employee theft is a problem of people—a problem of managers and their employees. Both managers and employees have an obligation to deter employee theft. Instilling ethics in an organization is an important process in deterring employee theft. Ethics enhances an individual and an organization. As people and their organizations are enhanced—as the culture becomes one of pride and honesty—employee theft will be deterred.

NOTES

1. "Light-fingered Work Ethics," *Time*, June 23, 1986, p. 64.

2. James D. Walls, Jr., "The Workplace: America's Hot Bed of Crime," *Vital Speeches of the Day*, April 1988, pp. 381–84.

3. "Notice Anything Missing Lately?" *Venture*, November 1988, p. 16.

4. Richard T. DeGeorge, *Business Ethics* (New York: Macmillan, 1986), p. 15.

5. Kenneth E. Goodpaster, "Some Avenues for Ethical Analysis in General Management," *Harvard Business School Note* 383–007, p. 6.

6. DeGeorge, *Business Ethics*, p. 32.

7. Immanuel Kant, *The Metaphysical Element of Justice* (New York: Library of Liberal Arts, 1965).

8. William J. Kehoe, "Ethics for Banking," *VBA Banking News*, December 1985, pp. 10–11.

9. John Stewart Mill, *Utilitarianism* (1863; reprint, Indianapolis: Bobbs-Merrill, 1957).

10. T. L. Beauchamp and N. E. Bowie, *Ethical Theory and Business* (Englewood Cliffs, N.J.: Prentice-Hall, 1988), p. 18.

11. Ibid. p. 19.

12. Harry Bacas, "To Stop a Thief," *Nation's Business*, 75 (June 1987), p. 17.

13. "Honestly, Can We Trust You?" *Time*, January 23, 1989, p. 44.

14. "How to Keep 'em Honest," *Psychology Today*, November 1981, p. 53.

15. Charles R. Carson, *Managing Employee Honesty* (Los Angeles: Security World Publishing Company, 1977), p. 19.

CHAPTER 6

Employee Theft and Employee Relations Issues

Most employees are employed as "employees at will." The general rule of employment at will is that "all may dismiss their employees at will, be they many or few, for good cause, for no cause, or even for cause morally wrong without being thereby guilty of legal wrong."[1] The relationship is grounded in mutuality—if the employee has the right to quit whenever he wants, then the employer must have the corresponding right to discharge the employee at any time. There are restrictions on this relationship, however.

Government regulation has prohibited many of the reasons employers formerly used to justify their discharge of employees. The National Labor Relations Act, one of the earliest forms of employer-employee regulation, prohibits employers from firing employees because of union or other activity protected by the Act.[2] Under the Occupational Safety and Health Act, an employer may not discharge or discriminate against an employee who has filed a complaint or who will testify in any occupational safety and health proceeding.[3] If employers receive federal funding or have government contracts over $2,500, they are prohibited from discriminating against or discharging certain disabled workers and must take affirmative action to employ and advance qualified disabled workers.[4] Likewise, employers with federal contracts for $10,000 or more must re-employ certain veterans.[5] Many federal statutes prohibit retaliation against employees who file complaints against their employers.[6] The

The material in this chapter is not intended to be an exhaustive discussion of employee theft and employment relations. It is an overview of the legal aspects of employee relations and is not intended as specific legal advice.

Bankruptcy Act prevents an employer from discharging an employee for declaring bankruptcy or for associating with an insolvent person.[7]

The principal federal acts that circumscribe discharge and discrimination are Title VII of the Civil Rights Act of 1964 (hereinafter Title VII),[8] the Civil Rights Act of 1866,[9] the Age Discrimination in Employment Act,[10] and the Fair Labor Standards Act (which includes the Equal Pay Act).[11] Executive Order 11246, which is applicable to federal contractors with contracts over $10,000, prohibits discrimination on the basis of race, color, religion, sex, and national origin, and has been interpreted to go beyond Title VII.[12]

Title VII prohibits employment discrimination on the basis of race, color, religion, sex, or national origin. Employer conduct is discriminatory if it is based on these factors and if it entails "the fail[ure] or refus[al] to hire or to discharge any individual with respect to his compensation, terms, conditions, or privileges of employment,"[13] and "limit[ing], segregat[ing], or classify[ing] his employees or applicants for employment in any way which would deprive or tend to deprive any individual of employment opportunities or otherwise adversely affect his status as an employee."[14] Discrimination on the basis of sex includes sexual harassment and discrimination on the basis of pregnancy, childbirth, or related medical conditions.[15] Employers are, however, allowed to distinguish between employees on the basis of a qualified seniority or merit system.[16] Employers may even hire and classify their employees on the basis of religion, sex, or national origin in those rare instances when these qualifications are reasonably necessary to operate a particular business.[17]

To avoid Title VII and other discrimination claims, employers should review their employment processes, from recruiting, interviewing, and hiring, to evaluations and disciplinary procedures, to termination procedures. The application, evaluation, discipline, and termination forms should be reviewed to ensure that they contain no forbidden categories.

The key to avoid discriminating against an applicant during the selection process is to keep your questions, inquiries, or comments to job-related areas. Questions appropriate for one job may be inappropriate for another. That is why preparation, knowledge of job and job requirements are extremely important. See Exhibit 6.1 for the subject and types of questions you want to avoid. Always remember in any exchange with an applicant that you are seeking job-related information.

Employers should establish policies to ensure that their supervisors and managers understand the prohibitions against discrimination. All employees, but managerial employees in particular, should understand the employer's policy against sexual harassment. Each employer should set up a procedure whereby employees who feel discriminated against or harassed have an opportunity to complain to someone—other than

Exhibit 6.1
Questions to Avoid

QUESTIONS TO AVOID	EXCEPTIONS & ALTERNATIVES
Race, national origin, religion, church attended, religious holidays.	You may and should ask if applicant is available to work his projected work schedule even if in response he brings up religious holidays.
Relative's birthplace, citizenship, etc.	After hire, your employee must complete an I-9 form which requires the employee to attest that he is a citizen or national, an alien lawfully admitted for permanent residence or an alien authorized by the Immigration and Naturalization Service to work in the United States.
Arrest Records	Arrest does not prove guilt; do not ask about arrests. However, on convictions, get details and consider nature of offense, relevance to job, how long ago offense occurred, subsequent behavior, etc. Make case-by-case determination, not across-the-board exclusion. Consult personnel department before excluding because of convictions. In some states it is unlawful to exclude for convictions over 10 years ago.
Children, child care arrangements, whether spouse objects to travel or night work.	Acceptable (and good idea) to ask if applicant would have any problem with projected work schedule and requirements including night work and travel, even if in response applicant brings up child care problems, spouse's objection, etc.
Marital status; future marital plans, pregnancy	Acceptable to ask after hire for tax, etc. purposes.
Age	You should inquire about and verify age if you suspect applicant is underage.
Credit rating, garnishment	Ask only if directly relevant to job duties; e.g., if job is in a position of trust over funds.
Labor Unions	May state the Company's position that it believes that unions have nothing constructive or worthwhile to offer the Company or its employees.
Handicap	After you have described the job to an applicant, you may inquire whether there are any physical or mental impairments that would prevent him or her from performing that job.
Military	May inquire if person served in military, job training received, etc. Do not ask what type of discharge was received.

the harasser—in a position of authority. Employers must be aware of off-color jokes, graffiti, suggestive comments, and any offensive physical contact. It is important that an employer react quickly and strongly to any rumor of discrimination or harassment.

Disgruntled employees are not only bringing suit under federal law, but also pushing the courts into recognizing new state-law claims. Many states are recognizing wrongful discharge claims against employers who have allegedly discharged employees in violation of public policy. These claims include retaliation for testifying in a case against the employer and discharge for complying with a jury summons. State courts also have accepted employment "contract" claims founded on the terms of employee handbooks, letters, and oral promises.

It is usually desirable for employers to keep their relationship with employees on an at-will basis. To do this it is essential that employers emphasize that the employee is an employee at will from the beginning of the employment relationship. The employee handbook should contain a prominent disclaimer stating that the handbook is not to be construed as a contract and does not alter the employee's status as an employee at will. The employer should reserve the right to change the handbook or to make exceptions to it at his discretion. The disclaimer also should state that oral statements contrary to the disclaimer are not effective unless they are reduced to writing and signed by an officer of the corporation.

PAPER-AND-PENCIL TESTS

Paper-and-pencil tests, which purport to measure honesty on a relative scale, should be scrutinized carefully before being used in the employment process. These tests can cause great resentment if used on current employees and may even raise invasion of privacy claims.[18] Even though honesty tests are legal in all states except Massachusetts, tests should not be used unless they have been validated in accordance with American Psychological Association Guidelines and the Equal Employment Opportunity Commission (EEOC) Uniform Guidelines on Employee Selection Procedures (1978).[19] The purpose of EEOC involvement in the testing area is to ensure that the tests do not discriminate on grounds of race, color, religion, sex, and national origin, but employers also should ensure that the test accurately measures traits that are relevant to the job. The tests should be constructed to minimize questions that intrude on a person's privacy, or that would require an employee or applicant to incriminate himself.

If your employees decide that your tests and testing methods have had a discriminatory impact on them, then they may sue you under Title VII.[20] Your employees will have to prove that the tests you give have an adverse impact on those who are protected by Title VII, and that there are other tests or selection devices that would serve the employer's legitimate interest in efficient and trustworthy workmanship without having an undesirable effect on people who are protected by Title VII. If an employer can prove, through validation studies and mandatory record keeping, that the tests are job-related and have not had a negative impact on protected classes, then the employer may be able to rebut the employees' claim. This kind of litigation is expensive and time-consuming, however, and one of the ramifications of which employers should be aware before they begin testing their applicants or employees.

If an employer chooses to implement paper-and-pencil tests, the employer should consider limiting those tests to applicants. Current employees resent the impersonality of a written test and may feel that such a test is an invasion of privacy. Applicants, on the other hand, have a lesser interest in privacy and usually are more willing to accept tests and other conditions for employment. Employers must make accommodations for those who cannot read, those who are blind or otherwise disabled, and those who cannot read, write, or speak English.[21]

Employers also must implement strict confidentiality and verification procedures, and must release the test results only to those within the employer's organization who have a legitimate need to know. Giving anyone else the test results on particular applicants or employees may open the door to a defamation or invasion of privacy suit.

Under some circumstances employee or applicant testing may be mandatory. More and more states are recognizing a legal cause of action titled "negligent hiring" and holding employers liable for the acts of their employees. If your business requires strict security, confidentiality, or trustworthiness in handling money or other sensitive situations, you should be particularly careful when hiring new employees.

POLYGRAPH TESTING

Polygraph tests are based on the principle that a conscious effort at deception produces involuntary physiological changes that are measurable and can be recorded on a graph.[22] The polygraph simultaneously records changes in such physiological processes as heartbeat, blood pressure, and respiratory rate,[23] through a pneumatic tube attached to the subject's abdomen or chest, a blood pressure cuff, and galvanic skin response sensors.[24]

There have long been arguments against polygraph tests, and in 1988 those opposed to the tests pushed the Polygraph Protection Act of 1988 through Congress. Critics of the polygraph claim that the inaccuracy of the tests have victimized untold numbers of honorable and truthful people.[25] There also have been studies that conclude that tongue biting, toe pressing, tranquilizers, and antiperspirants enable those who chose to deceive the polygraph to do so.[26]

With the passage of the Polygraph Protection Act of 1988 (hereinafter Polygraph Act), polygraph testing has been virtually eliminated from the private sector. State regulation also has imposed strictures on polygraph testing.[27] Therefore, even though there are some exceptions to the federal Polygraph Act, state regulation may circumscribe these exceptions.

The federal law exception afforded private employers is subject to strict regulation. Employers can give polygraph tests to employees only if the employer is conducting an "ongoing investigation."[28] The secretary of labor has declared that an "ongoing investigation" is of a specific incident or activity as opposed to random testing.[29] The employer must have a "reasonable suspicion that the employee was involved,"[30] and must explain in writing to the employee the specific incident being investigated and the basis for testing particular employees.[31] Furthermore, an employer can only test for specific economic injury to the employer's business—not long-term inventory loss and not theft committed by one employee against another.[32] Although employers involved in drug manufacturing and distribution and employers providing certain security services are allowed more leeway in polygraph testing, these employers also are subject to regulation.

Employers may not make a decision that affects an employee adversely, that is, discharge, discipline, deny promotion, or deny employment, solely on the basis of an analysis of a polygraph test chart or on an employee's refusal to take the test.[33] An employer also is prevented from disclosing the test results except to the employee taking the test, to people that the employee designates in writing, and to governmental agencies if the employee admits criminal conduct.[34]

Polygraph tests are expensive, often inaccurate, and subject to strict federal and state regulation. Employers who use polygraph tests are subject to wrongful discharge, invasion of privacy, defamation, and Polygraph Act suits. To deter legal liability, an employer should consult with its attorney before using polygraph tests.

SECURITY

Many employers do not realize that they have security problems until after theft or violence has occurred. It is important for employers to review their office layout and procedures for potential problems. For instance, where is the petty cash left? If everyone knows where the money is in the office, it not only makes stealing it a quick job, but also makes detecting the thief more difficult. If an employer does not have a sign-out program for tools and materials, the employer may have a difficult time avoiding "loss" of equipment and inventory.

Because most business owners are not security experts, it is usually worthwhile to have a security firm or consultant review your offices. It may seem like an expensive proposition, but it may save you money in inventory loss and theft.

REACTING TO THEFT

What do you do if you think an employee is stealing from the cash drawer? How should an employer react when its employees' pocket-books and desks are being rifled? What should an employer do if tools and supplies frequently are reported as "missing"? Although employers should react quickly to these situations, they should take the time to consider the full legal implications of their actions.

If you have a good idea which employee is stealing, you may choose to terminate that employee. Employers are not required to give their at-will employees the reasons for discharge, but if they do, the reasons must be truthful. Employers must choose their words of termination carefully. If an employer chooses not to reveal why it fires an employee, it should take into account the fact that if the employee files for un-employment compensation, it will have to either reveal the reason or acquiesce in paying the claim. Employers also should reflect on their civil duty to future employers of this employee and to the employee himself.

Employers should consider protective measures such as video mon-itoring, limiting access to certain areas of the office, stricter inventory control, and lock-and-key security for desks and pocketbooks. As dis-cussed earlier, these measures may cause some employee dissatisfaction and should be implemented only with employee participation.

An employer may choose to involve local law enforcement authorities. If the theft is particularly extensive and the employer suspects more than one employee, the employer should turn to someone whose job it is to solve crimes—most employers are not experts in criminal investigations. One option for employers is to report the theft and have the law en-forcement division conduct the entire investigation. Sometimes, if the case involves drugs or weapons, the police will be investigating your employees in connection with other charges. If this is the case, the police may be able to use the information you give them to arrest your em-ployees on other charges outside of your business establishment. This will protect you from unwanted publicity and claims that you helped the police violate the employees' civil rights.[35]

Employers also may participate with police in the investigation, hiring a "plant" for the office and perhaps even setting up a situation to tempt the thief. In this scenario a disgruntled employee has a good argument that the employer is acting "in concert" with the police and is, therefore, liable for any wrongful acts committed by the police. There also is the possibility of a dangerous or violent confrontation, however, and employers need to have the experience and authority of law enforcement officials readily available.

In deciding how to handle theft in the workplace, employers must consider other intangibles, such as unwanted publicity and the desired effect on current employees. Employees need to feel trusted and secure in the workplace. Employers must, however, guard against inventory loss and other theft. If managers confront rumors and reports of theft quickly and decisively, they should send the appropriate message to their employees.

PRIVACY RIGHTS OF EMPLOYEES

Search and Seizure

The Fourth Amendment of the U.S Constitution provides protection against unreasonable searches and seizures. This is only applicable, however, to public entities and those acting in concert with public entities. Nevertheless, even though private employers are constitutionally entitled to search their employees, employees may challenge the search under state law.[36] Employees may claim that the search invaded their privacy, and constituted false arrest and imprisonment, outrageous conduct, and assault and battery.[37]

Before proceeding, employers must carefully weigh the value of the search against the possible liability. A policy that has been posted and distributed to employees advising them of the circumstances of possible searches and the manner of those searches may deter some employees from bringing legal action. All supervisory employees should be familiar with the company policy and should be able to conduct a search in a nonthreatening and, hopefully, cooperative manner.

Disclosure of Personal Information

Defamation. Even though some employees may be offended at their employer's, or previous employer's, disclosure of unsavory employment facts, an employer usually is privileged to make such disclosures. Employers usually are protected by a qualified privilege that allows them to disseminate information about their employees as long as they do so in good faith and in response to inquiry from someone who has a legitimate need to know.[38]

Statements that imply that an employee has committed a crime or is untrustworthy may, however, be actionable.[39] To abrogate the qualified privilege, the plaintiff has to prove that the employer was motivated by malice or that the communication was not made to someone who did not have a legitimate interest in the matter. As one author put it, "ill-will sufficient to create an issue of fact for the jury on whether the qualified privilege has been abused may be inferred from only a few facts or a small amount of testimony, all of which may be from the mouth of the plaintiff. Qualified privilege hangs by a slender thread."[40]

Therefore, the best position for employers to take with regard to employee discharges and references is to give minimal information. When asked for a reference, most employers will only give the dates the employee worked for the employer, his or her position, and, if asked, whether the employer would rehire the employee. This may seem unfair to the prospective employer who is considering an employee who was fired for stealing, but each employer must decide how best to handle this type of situation. The primary drawback to disclosure is that former employees who were bad employees often look for retribution if they are unable to obtain other employment. If the employee was prosecuted, an option that every employer should consider when faced with theft, other employers will be able to obtain this information from public arrest records.

Invasion of Privacy. Although defamation claims are made to protect a person's interest in a good reputation, an invasion of privacy claim protects an employee's interest in being left alone. Employees most often allege that their employers unreasonably intruded into their private lives by publicly disclosing true, but embarrassing, private facts. These claims, like the defamation claims, occur when employers give unfavorable references to a prospective employer or release private information from personnel files. Other privacy claims have been brought for searches of personal possessions, wire tapping of private telephone conversations, and mandatory blood and urine tests. In all types of invasion of privacy claims the employee must prove that the employer's conduct is highly offensive to a reasonable person.

To avoid "disclosure of private fact claims," employers should review the procedures they have for handling personnel information. Employers should ensure that they are complying with all applicable state and federal laws. One good way to ensure compliance is to have your attorney and personnel manager set up a comprehensive policies and procedures manual. This manual should specify what type of records are kept and by whom, who has access to these records, and who has authority to disclose information. Employers should obtain signed release forms before disclosing information to anyone who is not in the employer's organization. Even with the consent form, employers should respond only to specific requests from a properly identified person who has a legitimate interest in the information. The employee in charge of personnel records should itemize the information released—a practice that deters improper disclosures and provides documentation for a legal defense.

Employees may resent the inconvenience and intrusion of searches, monitoring devices, and drug tests. This does not, however, give them a cognizable cause of action for invasion of privacy. If employees are forewarned about the possibility and procedure of searches, monitoring, and testing, these limited intrusions become conditions of continued employment with the employer. Employers should not force employees to submit to searches or testing, but employers should be prepared to discharge employees for failing to follow known company policies and procedures.

Monitoring systems, such as video cameras and keystroke counters, should be implemented with employee participation. Employers should explain to employees how, why, and when their work is being monitored. Many employers give their employees access to their own records, which, in some circumstances, improves productivity and encourages supervisory feedback. Employers should anticipate and allow for individual differences in productivity and should reasonably assess production standards. When installing video cameras, employers should be sensitive to employee privacy—restrooms and changing rooms should not be monitored.

THE IMPORTANCE OF DOCUMENTATION

More employment-related cases are lost because of nonexistent or poor documentation than for any other reason. Although documentation has always been important, it is becoming even more so as employees routinely challenge employment decisions before state and federal agencies and courts. Managers must remember that with most employment decisions, some employee or prospective employee will feel the adverse effects of that decision. Therefore, companies should consider the following guidelines in establishing sound, consistent documentation procedures.

Commitment of Senior Management

The president, chief executive officer, or owner of the company must be committed to and follow through on establishing sound documentation procedures throughout the organization. This may not make immediate dollar-and-cents sense, but as senior management sees the results of the unemployment compensation and other employment-related cases that are won, the time spent and effort expended by all levels of management in implementing good documentation procedures will be rewarded.

Commitment and Implementation by All Other Levels of Management

This factor is a must and speaks for itself. Although documentation might initially seem burdensome to managers, it soon becomes second nature.

Usable and Meaningful Forms

What do you want to achieve with a particular form? You want to secure relevant information for the specific employment decision in question. You want to be certain that the form makes sense to the people using it, managers and employees alike. A clear, concise form that succinctly obtains the needed information is preferable over a long, rambling form.

Reasonable Rules and Policies

Every employer should expect its employees to adhere to certain basic standards. It does no good for an employer to have his employees guess what those standards are. Employers should seriously consider adopting written guidelines and rules and then communicating those guidelines to each employee. Guidelines and rules must be tailored to your individual business needs, while complying with the many legal restrictions that exist. For example, how do you want to handle selecting employees for overtime and promotions? Choosing people at random can result in employee charges of favoritism, raises potential discrimination issues, and creates union issues in nonunion companies.

Supervisory Training

Supervisors have to have a solid understanding of all your guidelines and rules and how and for what purposes forms and documentation are to be used. Training is the key.

Audit Procedure to Ensure Consistency

Auditing the documents you have generated on your employees should help you in at least two ways. Auditing should assist you in monitoring the record you are making for each individual employee—to determine whether you are treating the employee in a manner consistent with the documents in the employee's file—and in ensuring that you are treating employees in similar situations in a similar manner.

You do not want to make a record for your employee that you will regret. For instance, if you suspect that an employee is taking tools home, you should do a specific investigation, and document that investigation for the employee's file. Remember, even if you have an "open file" policy, you do not have to disclose this type of information. You should, however, make sure that your policy provides for confidentiality and the nonrelease of investigatory information. If you suspect an employee of theft and want to separate the employee and the temptation by transferring the employee to another section or department, do not label the transfer a promotion. A promotion in your employee's file may cause you trouble when, if the problem continues, you choose to fire the employee. When you do terminate the employee, you can state as the "reason for termination" that the employee "violated company policy," or if you have sufficient evidence, you may choose to state the specific policy, such as "stealing company property." Remember, however, that an accusation of stealing can lead to suits for defamation and invasion of privacy.

Although two employment decisions seldom are alike because of variations in the facts, many are similar. For instance, habitual lateness might vary with the amount of time or days involved. In both instances, however, the employees are not punctual. It may be that your operation requires a great deal of teamwork, and one person's being late can throw a monkey wrench in your process. Your policy should provide a standard for punctuality, and when the employee exceeds that standard, whatever remedial or disciplinary procedures you adopt should be enforced. The same documents should be used to handle these similar situations. Periodic reviews that demonstrate widely varying treatment need to be investigated to determine the reason for the difference in treatment.

DISCIPLINE AND DISCHARGE

Unfortunately not every employee meets the reasonable expectations of the employer. When these situations occur, the employer needs to take corrective action, often of a disciplinary nature. When faced with these situations, employers should try to remember that they often have invested a significant amount of time, effort, and money in each employee. Turnover and the associated costs of hiring, orienting, and training new employees are unproductive costs that most employers want to avoid. Discipline that corrects the problem is preferable. The following are some guidelines that employers should consider as they develop and implement discipline and discharge procedures.

Policy Considerations

It is virtually impossible for an employer to list each and every rule a breach of which necessitates corrective and/or disciplinary action. Employers, however, can identify many matters that are likely to occur. Once an employer identifies these matters, it needs to communicate to each employee what they are and the likely consequences of the employee's refusal or inability to comply. Employers should review their selection of rules from a reasonableness viewpoint, asking themselves the following questions: (1) Do they reasonably help the employer to maintain a productive and safe workplace? (2) If challenged by the employee, how would a third party—like a judge, jury, or administrative agency—view the reasonableness of the rule? and (3) Does the corrective action or discipline taken fit the violation?

The Employee's Record

A review of the employee's personnel file is needed when any sort of corrective action is to be taken. Although you may think that you know the employee, a review of his or her file may help the manager more constructively deal with the employee problem.

Get the Facts

A thorough investigation should be conducted. Depending on the circumstances of the disciplinary matter, you may need to interview witnesses in addition to completely reviewing the employee's record. Determine how similar situations have been handled in the past. Understanding how those situations have been handled will help the manager be consistent as corrective action is taken in the case at hand.

Promptness

If a matter is such that corrective or disciplinary action is needed, it should be handled as quickly as possible. This does not mean, however, that a decision should be made at the expense of a thorough investigation. Employers should ensure that they have all the facts needed to make the proper decision.

The Follow-up

As with so many employment decisions, this step often can be the most important. The disciplined employee should be told what steps he or she needs to take to correct the problem. Do not leave the employee in limbo. Remember the time, money, and training you have invested in the employee. Positive feedback, if appropriate, may help to turn the employee into the productive person he or she can be. If the problem is a major transgression of company policy, however, the employer need not give at-will employees the reason for termination.

CONCLUSION

The purpose of this chapter is to offer general advice on matters of employee relations and to provide a framework for thinking about employee theft problems from the lawyer's perspective. We have included as Appendix 4 a list of "Dos and Don'ts in Dealing with Employee Theft." It was prepared by James P. McElligott, Jr., a partner with the law firm McGuire Woods Battle & Boothe in Richmond, Virginia.

NOTES

1. *Payne v. Western A.R.R. Co.*, 81 Tenn. 507 (1884).
2. 29 U.S.C. §151 *et seq.*
3. 29 U.S.C. §151 *et seq.*
4. Vocational Rehabilitation Act of 1973, 29 U.S.C. §794.
5. The Vietnam Era Veterans Readjustment Assistance Act, 38 U.S.C. §2012.
6. The Federal Mine Health and Safety Act, 30 U.S.C. §815(c), prevents an employer from discharging an employee for filing a complaint about mining safety or health; the False Claims Act, 31 U.S.C. §3730(h), protects employees who expose employer fraud against the federal government; the Surface Transportation Assistance Act of 1982, 23 U.S.C. §101 *et seq.*, prohibits employers from discharging employees of interstate trucking firms for complaints or for refusing to operate an unsafe truck; the Comprehensive Environmental Response Compensation and Liability Act of 1980, 42 U.S.C. §9601 *et seq.*, prevents the discharge or discrimination against any employee complaining about or testifying about hazardous substances; the Employee Retirement Income Security Act of 1973, 29 U.S.C. §1140, prohibits the discharge of an employee who challenges a decision about employee medical, retirement, or other benefits.
7. 11 U.S.C. §525(b).
8. 42 U.S.C. §2000e *et seq.*
9. 42 U.S.C. §1981.
10. 29 U.S.C. §621 *et seq.*
11. 29 U.S.C. §201 *et seq.*
12. 30 Fed. Reg. 12319 (1965).
13. 42 U.S.C. §2000e–2(a)(1).
14. 42 U.S.C. §2000e–2(a)(2).
15. 42 U.S.C. §2000e(k).
16. 42 U.S.C. §2000e–2(e)(h).
17. 42 U.S.C. §2000e–2(e).
18. Courts have traditionally held that current employees have a more legit-

imate expectation of privacy than do applicants for employment. James A. Douglas, Daniel E. Feld, and Nancy Asquith, *Employment Testing Manual*, 14–2 (Boston: Warren, Gorham & Lamont, 1989).

19. 29 C.F.R. 1607 (1989). The Equal Employment Opportunity Commission requires one of the following three types of validation studies:

1. Criterion-related validity studies showing through empirical data that the selection procedure is predictive of or significantly correlated with important elements of job performance

2. Content validity studies showing that the content of a selection procedure is representative of important aspects of performance on the job

3. Construct validity studies showing that the procedure measures the degree to which candidates have identifiable characteristics that have been determined to be important in successful performance in the job

20. 42 U.S.C. §2000(e) *et seq.*

21. If literacy, sight, physical ability, and/or English-language ability are necessary for adequate job performance, an employer may exclude these people. The employer must be certain, however, that it has made an attempt to reasonably accommodate disabled workers.

22. Douglas, Feld, and Asquith, *Employment Testing Manual*, 13–3.

23. *The American Heritage Dictionary*, 2nd ed. (Boston: Houghton-Mifflin Company, 1982), p.961.

24. Douglas, Feld, and Asquith, *Employment Testing Manual*, 13–3.

25. Arnold Lykken, "The Case Against the Polygraph in Employment Screening," *Personnel Administrator*, 30 (September 1985), p. 59.

26. Douglas, Feld, and Asquith, *Employment Testing Manual*, 13–5 to 13–6.

27. According to one author, thirty states regulate the use of lie detector tests. Douglas, Feld, and Asquith, *Employment Testing Manual*, A–83 to A–99 (summarizing state laws regulating lie detector tests).

28. Employee Polygraph Protection Act of 1988, Pub. L. No. 100–347, §7.

29. 29 C.F.R. §801.12(b).

30. Ibid.

31. 29 C.F.R. §801.12(a)(4).

32. 29 C.F.R. §801.12(b) and (c)(3).

33. 29 C.F.R. §801.20, 801.21.

34. 29 C.F.R. §801.35.

35. 42 U.S.C. §1983 allows civil rights suits against the police and against a private employer if the employer acts in concert with the police.

36. See *Burdeau v. McDowell*, 256 U.S. 465, 41 S.Ct. 571 (1921).

37. In a challenge to a search of an employee's vehicle, the employee charged invasion of privacy, false arrest and imprisonment, outrageous conduct, and reckless and wanton disregard by the employer of the employee's right to be left alone. *Gretencord v. Ford Motor Co.*, 538 F.Supp. 331(D.Kan. 1982). The court found that no intrusion had taken place because the employee had refused the search. If employees are under a collective bargaining agreement, suits under state law may be pre-empted by federal labor law. See *Penrith v. Lockheed Corp.*, 1 IER Cases 760 (D.Calif. 1986) (denying plaintiff right to proceed on claims of

false arrest and imprisonment, assault and battery, invasion of privacy, breach
of fiduciary duty, negligence, negligent hiring and wrongful discharge for search
of employee's vehicle on employer's premises, and subsequent arrest, suspen-
sion, and discharge).

38. W. Page Keeton, et al., *Prosser and Keeton on the Law of Torts*, §115 at 27.
5th ed., 1984.

39. See *Bobenhauser v. Cassat Avenue Mobile Homes Inc.*, 344 So.2d 279 (Fla.
Dist. Ct. App. 1977) (former employer liable for telling prospective employer
that discharged employee was a "thief and a crook"); *Roqozinski v. Air Stream
by Angell*, 152 N.J. Super. 133, 377 A.2d 807 (1977) (former employer told unemployment compensation board that employee "had to be continually
watched," but court found that employer was not liable because he had no
improper motive); *Cook v. Safeway Stores*, 266 Ore. 77, 511 P.2d 375 (1973) (manager told three other employees that former employee had been fired for stealing.

40. William J. Holloway and Michael J. Leech, *Employment Termination* (Washington, D.C.: Bureau of National Affairs, Inc., 1985), pp. 323–24.

CHAPTER 7

Using Internal Controls to Reduce Employee Theft

As we have well established, the effects of employee theft on firms can be devastating. Because of the competitive nature of the markets they serve and the financial constraints they face, small businesses in particular can ill afford to ignore this problem. As stated previously, one estimate suggests that almost one-third of all business failures in the United States are due to internal theft. Interestingly, most small-business owners are not sensitive enough to the threat posed by this form of theft, and tend to regard it as a cost of doing business. Internal issues in general and employee theft in particular tend to be ignored unless and until severe problems arise.

All business managers need to understand more about employee theft so that they can take steps to correct the problem. As a first step, several myths need to be exposed:

Myth: Most employees will not steal. In fact, studies have shown that most employees are susceptible to the temptation to steal. And those who do steal come from all social classes and economic circumstances.

Myth: Theft losses are not material. The large magnitude of losses nationwide has already been noted. On an individual theft basis, studies show that although initial thefts may involve insignificant amounts, they tend to continue and to grow larger.

Myth: Most thefts go undetected. Studies have shown that most thieves become careless and are discovered. Many are simply revealed by accident, others are reported by co-workers, and the rest are uncovered by internal controls and audits.[1] Knowing the great impact that employee theft can have on businesses and that actions can be taken to reduce it, managers and owners are in a position to improve both the organizational climate in their businesses and their profits.

THE IMPORTANCE OF INTERNAL CONTROLS

The implementation of appropriate internal control procedures is a fundamental and important step in reducing employee theft. Controls can minimize errors and mistakes in transactions and record keeping. For example, inadvertent errors in orders to suppliers and in billings to customers—which can "steal" profits—can be prevented by appropriate controls. Controls also can safeguard assets such as cash and inventory that are easily misappropriated. Furthermore, good controls can reduce the work of external auditors, decrease their billings, and increase profits.

To be effective, the controls used and the way they are implemented must reflect an understanding of who is likely to steal from the company and how he or she might do it. Three factors are present in virtually all instances of employee theft: (1) a motive—usually a financial need because of external obligations; (2) a perceived opportunity to steal without detection; and (3) an ability to rationalize the theft—usually by thinking of it as something else, such as "what's due me." Internal controls can limit the second factor by increasing the probability of detection, thereby providing a deterrent to theft. It is not sufficient, however, just to design internal controls; they also must be enforced. Furthermore, internal control procedures must be used in a consistent manner, and they should not differentiate among owners, managers, partners, officers, relatives, or friends.

ORGANIZATIONAL CLIMATE AND CONTROL OF THEFT

Effective internal control begins with the creation of a climate within the organization that supports and reinforces such values as honesty and integrity. As we have stated previously, effective communication with employees is critical. It is important to give employees an understanding of the company's objectives and strategies. Employees should have the perception that the company is well run and that its owners and managers care about ethical conduct. The company should consider having a written code of conduct that addresses legal and ethical behavior conflicts of interest, what constitutes theft, and related issues. It should be distributed to employees upon initial employment, and reviewed with them periodically thereafter. Everyone should understand what constitutes theft and what the consequences will be for those committing the offense.

Including in employee evaluations the degree of compliance with the company's code of conduct and with established internal controls can reinforce these values. Employees also can be motivated to adhere to the company's values through other motivators, such as operating reports, internal financial reports, budgets, and variance analyses.[2] Again, it is essential for all members of the management team to adhere closely to these values. If managers deviate from the values even slightly, the employees may conclude that these values are mere window dressing. The creation of an appropriate climate in the firm is thus a necessary precondition for the effective implementation of internal control procedures.

ASSESSING RISK OF EMPLOYEE THEFT

Before planning and implementing internal controls, managers should assess the degree of risk of employee theft in their companies. Higher risks are associated with those companies that have the following characteristics:

- Relatively large amounts of cash are handled
- Responsibility for operations and assets are concentrated in relatively few employees
- Supervision of employees is lax
- Employees perceive that management lacks a concern for integrity
- Record keeping is lax (i.e., records are nonexistent or are not kept up-to-date)
- Reconciliation of checking accounts to bank statements is lax
- Documents such as invoices and purchase orders are not serially numbered
- Employee morale is low
- Employee turnover tends to be high, particularly in the accounting department
- Employee salaries and/or salary increases are relatively low
- Payrolls are not met on a timely basis

These and similar conditions provide employees with both opportunity and motive to engage in theft. Companies with such characteristics have higher risks of employee theft than companies without them.

Exhibit 7.1 list specific "indicators" that may point to potential or

Exhibit 7.1
Indicators That Often Accompany Employee Theft

- Customers complaining about their account balances
- Failure or refusal of employees to take earned leaves
- Changes in employees' life-styles, particularly increases in extravagance
- Excessive transactions involving cash
- Excessive use of traveler's checks or cashier's checks
- Excessive changes in write-offs of uncollectible accounts receivable (i.e., bad debts)
- Unexplained adjustments to inventory balances
- Unexplained adjustments to accounts receivable balances
- Second endorsements on checks
- Unusual endorsements on checks
- Missing documents, such as canceled checks, invoices, and debit and credit memoranda
- Photocopies of invoices in files rather than originals
- Old items in bank reconciliations
- Old outstanding checks that have not cleared the bank
- Unusual patterns in deposits in transit to the bank
- Questionable changes in financial ratios, particularly those involving inventory and net income

Sources: W. Steve Albrecht, "How CPAs Can Help Clients Prevent Employee Fraud," *Journal of Accountancy*, December 1988, pp. 110–14; Marvin M. Levy, "Financial Fraud: Schemes and Indicia," *Journal of Accountancy*, August 1985, pp. 78–87.

existing employee theft that demands immediate attention. These indicators, by themselves, do not prove that theft exists, but they often are present when theft occurs. For example, many theft schemes require constant, careful monitoring by the perpetrator. Concealment often involves manipulation of accounting records and/or supporting documentation. Taking earned leaves, such as vacations or extended holidays, increases the likelihood that a replacement employee will discover a cash shortage or an alteration of the company's records to conceal the theft. Therefore, employees engaged in theft often volunteer to forego their leaves "for the good of the company."

USING INTERNAL CONTROLS

Once these basic questions and issues have been addressed, it is important to focus attention on the specific controls needed to minimize the incidence of employee theft. Careless or inadequate internal controls provide an attractive inducement to would-be thieves, and they suggest that management is not serious about the problem. Good internal controls, on the other hand, can help to increase productivity by minimizing waste, unintentional errors, and fraud. In addition, internal controls make it difficult for dishonest employees to flourish by increasing the odds that a thief will be caught.

As previously established, controls are useful but can be detrimental to a business when used to excess. A tightly controlled environment can have the adverse effect of reducing both productivity and creativity. Finding the appropriate level of internal control, therefore, is a critical management responsibility that requires the use of good judgment. In small businesses, in particular, the job can be especially difficult for two reasons: not enough staff and too little money.

GENERAL CONSIDERATIONS IN DESIGNING CONTROLS

Virtually all internal controls involve dividing employee responsibilities three ways: (1) authorization of transactions, with supporting documentation of approval; (2) physical custody of assets, with periodic reconciliation to the company's records; and (3) timely record keeping, with supporting documentation to detect errors or theft. If a single employee has two or all three of these responsibilities, the opportunities for theft and concealment are significantly increased. Therefore, in designing internal controls for a company, these responsibilities should be separated, if at all possible.

The first step in planning a control system is to study the company's operations thoroughly. The flow of assets—particularly liquid assets like cash, securities, and some inventories—must be traced. Likewise, the flow of documentation and record keeping must be carefully identified. Then questions such as these must be asked: Where are there particular weaknesses, that is, where are the "weak spots"? How could theft take place and be hidden? What could go wrong? What controls are needed?

In carrying out this evaluation, the focus should be on the key cycles of the company's operations: the revenue or income-producing cycle, the cost of sales or production cycle, the financing cycle, and nonroutine transactions. The "informal" system should be considered as well as the formal one. For example, who is responsible for authorization, physical custody, or record keeping when the primary employees are at lunch, on vacation, and so on? Useful tools for this evaluation include internal control checklists, flow charting, "walk throughs," sampling, and risk exposure worksheets.

The following are examples of things that could go wrong in the revenue cycle:

✓ • Credit could be granted inappropriately
- Sales could be made to unapproved customers
- Orders could be accepted that could not be filled
- Sales could go unrecorded or be recorded in error
- Billings to customers could be made in error
- Collections from customers could be misappropriated or mishandled
- Cash sales receipts could be misappropriated or mishandled
- Collections could go unrecorded or be recorded in error
- Returns and allowances could be granted or recorded in error[3]

Electronic data processing (EDP), that is, computers, poses a special challenge in designing control systems. A detailed treatment of this technical area is beyond the scope of this book. It should be noted, however, that when a system is computerized, the separation of duties (transaction authorization, asset custody, and record keeping) often is compromised. Consequently the risk of employee theft increases. In evaluating a computer-based system it is wise to consider the EDP system as if it represented a single employee, because one key employee with access to the system would be able to control documentations and operations flowing through the system. Establishing strong input and user review controls, requiring access controls such as passwords, and maintaining a log of employee processing can establish responsibility for specific EDP functions.

An expert in internal control systems has observed:

> The key to maintaining adequate segregation of responsibilities, in spite of central processing by EDP, is to assign input and output control responsibilities to non-EDP personnel, to keep tight control over highly exposed processing activities such as the computerized printing and signing of checks, and to clearly delineate job responsibilities within the EDP department, maintaining file access controls and efficiently incorporating edit checks for propriety, accuracy, and completeness of processing activities. These compensating controls . . . can lead to an adequate system of control with respect to segregation of duties.[4]

The controls selected for a company must be tailor-made for its own environment and conditions, giving due consideration to number of employees, their duties, the degree of computerization, potential weak spots, and so on. Appendix 5 is a checklist that can be used to identify controls that may be appropriate in various areas of a company's operations. This checklist, developed by Neil H. Snyder, O. Whitfield Broome, Jr. and Karen Zimmerman for a research project investigating the use of internal controls to reduce employee theft, is the most complete one available.

SPECIAL CONSIDERATION FOR SMALL BUSINESSES

Identifying the controls that are essential to reduce theft in smaller businesses is critically important.[5] In dealing with the theft problem a smaller firm must come to grips with severe constraints that a larger firm does not encounter. And, as a result of these constraints and the different needs of a small business, the firm's survival may depend on a successful control system. With these considerations in mind, the following discussion gives attention to the identification of specific internal control procedures that should be in place in any small business.

METHODOLOGY USED TO IDENTIFY CONTROLS FOR SMALL BUSINESSES

Differentiating Between Small, Medium, and Large Businesses

To focus on the particular needs of small businesses, reliance was placed on the work of Donald Thain, who developed criteria for differentiating between small, medium, and large businesses. For example, smaller firms, according to Thain, face different kinds of problems than the others. They tend to have different objectives and strategies for achieving them, tend to organize differently, and tend to use different decision processes. Thain's work was summarized and then expert evaluators (described below) were asked to use this information as a guide in attempting to differentiate, consistently and objectively, among small, medium, and large firms in regard to their internal control needs.

Developing a Comprehensive List of Internal Controls

Identifying the internal controls that might be used by small businesses to reduce employee theft necessitated gathering information from various sources. Using the information from these sources, a control checklist was prepared. This list of controls is believed to be the most comprehensive currently available.

Identifying Controls That All Small Businesses Should Use

Eight certified public accountants (CPAs) were asked to serve as expert evaluators in identifying controls that should be used by all small businesses. Four of the CPAs were partners in large international accounting firms, and the other four were partners in local or regional firms.

CPAs were thought to be an ideal choice for this job because they are viewed widely by people in the business community as knowledgeable, thorough, morally upright, ethical, honest, and objective. Also, no other group in our society is likely to know more about the appropriate use of internal controls than CPAs. The fact that only eight CPAs were asked to assist in this research represents a constraint on the ability to generalize from the findings. Each CPA who worked on the project, however, contributed up to twenty hours of time to provide the information needed. This substantial time requirement accounts for the decision to use a small number of evaluators.

Each of the expert evaluators was instructed to use the criteria in Thain's matrix to develop an understanding of the particular control needs of small businesses and then to identify the specific controls that should be used by small businesses to reduce employee theft.

In explaining the purpose of this research to the CPAs, it was noted that small-business owners might be relatively uninformed about the importance of internal controls in reducing employee theft. Consequently they might overlook controls as a viable option for dealing with the theft problem. Without exception, the CPAs shared this opinion, and most of them provided anecdotal information that supported it. Additionally, most of the CPAs believed that smaller businesses are different enough to justify giving them special consideration in the formulation of internal control procedures.

RESULTS OF THE STUDY

It is unusual for eight professional people to agree on any issue, including the importance of various internal controls. Therefore, only those controls that were identified by six or more (75 percent or more) of the expert evaluators as being important have been defined as essential for small businesses.

As mentioned previously, implementing controls costs money, and controls that provide little or no benefit should be avoided. It was thought desirable, however, to exercise caution in recommending that a control not be used because of the possibility that it might have value in some particular types of small businesses. Therefore, the only controls classified as unnecessary for small businesses were those controls that were unanimously identified by the expert evaluators as being unimportant.

The findings of this research are presented in Exhibit 7.2. Individual controls are classified as being related to cash, payroll, investments, inventories, general business, accounts and notes receivable, accounts payable, sales, or property, plant, and equipment, in that order. Only the controls that were identified by six or more of the expert evaluators as important, or by all of them as unimportant, are included in the results for the reasons previously stated.

Exhibit 7.2
Essential Controls and Unnecessary Controls for Small Businesses

CONTROL CATEGORY

Cash

1. A record of all cash receipts should be made by cash register tapes, counter sales slips, etc.	KR—E
2. The mail should be opened by a person having no access to cash receipts records.	KR—E
3. Each day's cash receipts should be deposited intact promptly.	SA—E
4. The firm should have a policy forbidding the cashing of checks from daily cash receipts.	KR—E
5. A specific person should be responsible for cash from the time of receipt until it is deposited.	RE—E
6. Cash receipts should be deposited without delay if the names of customers are not readily determinable.	KR—E
7. All customers, checks returned by the bank should be followed up for subsequent disposition.	DE—E
8. A permanent copy of each issued receipt should be maintained.	KR—E
9. Prenumbered invoices should be prepared for all cash sales over the counter.	KR—E
10. All customers' checks should be restrictively endorsed immediately on receipt.	SA—E
11. All firm checks should be prenumbered and periodically accounted for.	SA—E
12. All payments should be made by check or from a petty cash fund.	KR—E
13. Firm policy should prohibit the signing or co-signing of checks in advance.	DE—E
14. The use of unnumbered "counter" checks should be forbidden.	SA—E
15. Supporting documents should accompany all checks submitted for signature.	SA—E
16. The checkbook should be balanced and the total maintained in agreement with the cash account in the general ledger.	KR—E

Exhibit 7.2 (continued)

CONTROL CATEGORY

---

17. All payments from petty cash should be adequately supported by evidence.   KR—E

18. A petty cash fund should be established for a fixed amount, placed under the control of a specific employee, and reimbursed only on presentation of documents supporting valid expenditures.   RE—E

19. Cash receipts from customers should be totally segregated from the petty cash fund.   RE—E

20. The dollar amount of petty cash transactions should be checked periodically for reasonableness.   DE—E

21. Access to the petty cash fund should be restricted to the employee responsible for the fund.   RE—E

22. Surprise audits of cash receipts should be made periodically.   IO—U

23. All petty cash vouchers supporting payments should be filled out in ink.   IO—U

Payroll

1. The time of hourly employees on the payroll should be supported by approved time cards or other records.   KR—E

2. All salaries and wages should be paid by check.   DE—E

3. Signed receipts should be obtained for any cash payments to employees.   KR—E

4. Receipts supporting payments to employees should be cancelled promptly to prevent reuse.   DE—E

5. A separate personnel department should maintain complete personnel records, including wage and salary data.   SI—U

6. Independent timekeepers should be used to assure correct employee time reporting.   SI—U

7. Production reports should be used to assure correct employee time reporting.   SI—U

8. Labor distribution tickets should be independently computed and tabulated to provide an independent check on aggregate pay.   SI—U

9. Departmental distributions for salaries and wages should be carefully made, checked, and approved by an accounting official.   SI—U

Exhibit 7.2 (continued)

CONTROL CATEGORY

---

10. If incentive wage systems are used, production reporting should be independently checked against production or sales data periodically. IO—U

11. If incentive wage systems are used, standards should be periodically reviewed to compare them with time wage rates. IO—U

Investments

1. Securities should be kept under lock and key or in a safe deposit box. SA—E

2. A record should be kept of each security, including certificate number. KR—E

3. Securities should be registered in the name of the company. SA—E

Inventories

1. All inventory on premises should be physically counted at least once each year. DE—E

2. All inventory off premises should be confirmed or physically counted at least once each year. DE—E

3. Physical counts of inventory at year-end should be conducted under the supervision of a responsible official. DE—E

4. Inventories stored in public warehouses should be physically checked from time to time. DE—E

5. Properly authorized, receipted requisitions should be required for all withdrawals of inventory from storerooms. SI—U

6. Perpetual inventory records should be periodically checked with inventory in stock by persons independent of the inventory records. SI—U

7. Written instructions should be prepared to guide employees counting inventory at year end. IO—U

8. Summaries of detailed inventory sheets for year-end inventories should be double-checked. SI—U

9. The employee responsible for purchasing inventory should be independent of the receiving and disbursing functions. SI—U

10. All inventory purchase orders should be prepared on the basis of purchase requisitions or production schedules prepared by other departments. SI—U

11. Expenditures for major services or inventory purchases should be approved by the board of directors. SI—U

Exhibit 7.2 (continued)

CONTROL CATEGORY

---

12. A responsible employee should establish the distribution of purchase and expense items.   IO—U

13. A responsible employee should review the prices paid for inventory to determine that they are not in excess of market.   IO—U

14. Purchase orders in excess of prescribed limits should be approved by someone other than the employee placing the order.   IO—U

General

1. Employees who handle cash and/or securities should have their duties assigned to others during the vacation period.   DE—E

2. All entries in the books of account should be supported by original journal entries.   KR—E

3. All bank accounts in the name of the company should be recorded in the books of account.   KR—U

4. All journal entries should be approved by a person other than the one preparing the entries.   IO—U

5. A current organization chart should be maintained.   SI—U

6. The chief accounting officer should report to a responsible official.   SI—U

7. The company should have an internal auditor.   SI—U

8. The internal auditor should report to a responsible official.   SI—U

Accounts and Notes Receivable

1. Customers' accounts should be balanced regularly with the receivables account in the general ledger.   KR—E

2. Monthly statements should be sent to all customers.   DE—E

3. Write-offs of bad debts should be authorized by a responsible official.   DE—E

4. Notes receivable and renewals of notes should be authorized by a responsible official.   DE—E

5. Monthly customers' statements should be independently checked with customers' accounts and mailed by someone other than the accounts receivable bookkeeper.   SI—U

6. Accounts receivable bookkeepers should be rotated among various customers' accounts receivable ledgers from time to time.   SI—U

7. The custodian of notes receivable should be independent of employees receiving cash or recording transactions.   IO—U

Accounts Payable

1. The individual accounts payable accounts should be balanced regularly with the general ledger accounts payable account.   KR—E

Exhibit 7.2 (continued)

CONTROL CATEGORY

---

2. When processing items for payment, terms, prices, and quantities on invoices should be checked against purchase orders.   DE—E

3. Amounts for disputed items should be entered in the accounts, and the invoices should be maintained in a separate file.   IO—U

Sales

1. The billing department should be entirely separate from the accounts receivable and shipping departments.   SI—U

2. Confirmations of orders should be regularly sent to customers.   IO—U

3. Exceptions to standard pricing should be approved in writing by a responsible official in the sales department.   IO—U

Property, Plant, and Equipment

1. Property, plant, and equipment items should be identified by number.   IO—U

Codes:

KR—keeping records

DE—duties of employees

SA—securing assets   E—essential

RE—responsibility of employees   U—unnecessary

IO—involvement of owner or manager

SI—size insufficient

ANALYSIS OF RESULTS

The opinions of the expert evaluators led to the identification of forty-two controls as essential for small businesses. As might be expected, most of these controls—twenty-one—relate to cash, the most liquid asset and the one most susceptible to theft. Of the remaining essential controls, from two to four each relate to payroll, investments, inventories, general business, accounts and notes receivable, and accounts payable.

Types of Essential Controls

In considering the use of these controls the small-business owner or manager may find it useful to group them into a few categories that describe their general nature or purpose. In this study four categories have been used that classify the essential controls by common techniques of safeguarding assets or assuring accuracy. These are keeping records, duties of employees, securing assets, and responsibility of employees. It is possible that a control may be related to more than one classification, but for current purposes each control is included only in the most logical category.

Keeping Records. Some controls are directed toward establishing records that provide a check on employees' handling of assets and transactions. If possible, therefore, record keeping should be performed by people who do not have custody of the asset in question or responsibility for the transaction being controlled. This separation may be difficult to achieve in small businesses. In Exhibit 7.2 the controls that involve record keeping are designated by the letters KR.

Duties of Employees. Another type of control involves the delegation of tasks to employees so that the duties of one serve as a check on the activities of another. Controls that require approval by an owner or manager to complete a transaction also fit into this category, as do controls that involve checks by people outside the business. Involving customers in assuring that salespeople correctly record the amount of a sale by way of a cash register or a receipt is one example of the latter control. In Exhibit 7.2 controls of this type are identified by the letters DE.

Securing Assets. Securing assets under lock and key or securing them off-premises represents another type of control. Using checks rather than cash to pay bills is a way of controlling cash by placing it in the custody of a bank off-premises. Assets also can be secured other than physically, such as by prenumbering checks, registering securities, and using restrictive endorsements. The letters SA are used in Exhibit 7.2 to identify these controls.

Responsibility of Employees. Finally, controls may be classified as those that clearly place responsibility for an asset with a single employee. In Exhibit 7.2 this type of control is identified by the letters RE.

Unnecessary Controls

The CPAs who served as expert evaluators in this study did not explain why they considered some of the internal controls in the checklist to be unimportant for small businesses. They did unanimously agree, however, that thirty-two of the controls were unimportant. An analysis of these controls leads to inferences about the types of controls that small businesses may not find practical or cost-effective. Two categories have been used in this connection: involvement of owner or manager (IO in Exhibit 7.2) and size insufficient (SI in Exhibit 7.2). It should be noted, however, that these two categories are closely related, and most of the unnecessary controls can be included in both of them.

Involvement of an Owner or Manager. In smaller businesses owners or managers are typically closely involved on a daily basis. Furthermore, the scope of operation of most small businesses permits the owner or manager to be involved in many or most aspects of the business. Thus he or she can provide the control, rather than establishing a costly procedure or structure to do it.

Size Insufficient. Many small businesses have too few employees to make certain controls possible, practical, or cost-effective. Therefore, the owner or manager must be aware of the absence of these controls and substitute personal involvement for them.

Using these results from the CPAs who served as expert evaluators of internal controls, small-business owners and managers should be able to take steps to control employee theft.

EXAMPLES OF EMPLOYEE THEFT AND RELATED CONTROLS

The following cases provide examples of employee theft schemes and suggest internal controls that can be used to prevent or detect such thefts.[6] These are only a few examples of employee theft and by no means are intended to constitute an all-inclusive list. As discussed above, each business must evaluate its own operations and environment to determine where employee theft is most likely and what controls to implement.

Bogus Checks to Vendors. An employee who had responsibility for authorizing checks approved the preparation of checks to the company's regular vendors based on fake invoices and receiving reports he had supplied. After the checks were prepared he had them returned to himself for transmittal to the vendors. He then forged the vendors' endorsements on the back of the checks, added his own endorsement, and deposited them to his account. On the company's records the checks were recorded as valid purchases of inventory and, ultimately, included in cost of goods sold expense.

Internal controls that would mitigate this theft include prohibiting signed checks from being returned to the authorizer or to the signer for disposition. In addition, the employee in charge of performing bank reconciliations should be charged with examining the backs of cancelled checks for double endorsements.

Lapping. A common but complicated defalcation scheme is known as "lapping." An employee responsible for receiving and recording customers' payments on account stole the payments—either by taking cash or forging endorsements on customers checks—and made no entries. Future payments from customers were used to make up the missing reductions in customers' accounts. Even with the assistance of a microcomputer, this scheme eventually became so complicated that the employee could not continue to cover all of the missing reductions. The theft was discovered when customers complained. In the meanwhile, however, the company had lost the cash.

In designing internal controls the employee responsible for receiving the cash should not also have access to accounts receivable balances. Sending regular (e.g., monthly) statements of account to customers—prepared by an employee other than one responsible for receipt of payments—can uncover such theft on a timely basis. Periodic (at least annual) confirmation with customers of their account balances also is a desirable control.

Forging and Concealing Checks. In a small company an employee was responsible for keeping the company's books and for preparing the bank reconciliation at the end of the month. She was able to take checks from an unused checkbook, write checks to herself, forge the authorized signature, and cash the checks. To conceal the theft she "misfooted" the disbursements journal to indicate more cash spent than the details supported. An offsetting "misfooting" added the cash stolen to the inventory purchases column. When the forged checks were returned by the bank, she destroyed them.

The control system should clearly provide for separation of record keeping, bank reconciliation, and custody of unused checks among different employees. If the company is too small for such separation of duties, either the owner or an outsider (such as an auditor) should be responsible for reconciling the bank statement with the company's cash account monthly. Alternatively, the owner may request "cutoff" bank statements, accompanied by copies of cancelled checks, to be sent to the external auditor several times each year.

Falsifying Payroll Records. An employee responsible for the preparation of the payroll created "ghost" employees, added them to the payroll, claimed their checks, and then endorsed and cashed them. The cash stolen was, therefore, charged to compensation expense. In large businesses with many employees these "ghosts" may be difficult to identify.

Again, separation of responsibilities is a key control in this case. Responsibility for adding and deleting names from the payroll should reside with an employee who has no access to the payroll checks. This theft often can be discovered by examining Social Security numbers and comparing them with a list of numbers actually issued by the government or by obtaining lists of employees who are not participating in company fringe benefit plans.

Petty Cash Theft. An employee responsible for a petty cash fund misappropriated relatively small amounts and covered the thefts by false receipts and other documentation for office supplies, meals for overtime workers, and cab fares.

Internal control over petty cash funds should include surprise counts by another employee, such as a supervisor, at irregular intervals. At any time the sum of the cash in the fund and the receipts for payments should equal the fixed total of the fund. When a petty cashier is suspected of theft, the fund can be counted twice in one day. Theft also may be detected by analyzing payments by purpose over a period of time and looking for unusual patterns.

CONCLUSION

To reduce employee theft, owners and managers must first and foremost establish an atmosphere of honesty and integrity within their business and personally set a standard for their employees to follow. They should evaluate their own environment to determine where employee theft is most likely to occur. In doing so, they should ask questions such as: Have we created an environment for effective control? Are control and operating responsibilities appropriately segregated? Have appropriate checks and balances been established? Are all transactions being recorded in the accounting system? This evaluation will lead to the selection of controls, such as those contained in Exhibit 7.2, that pertain to their business and its structure.

It is important that owners and managers monitor the operation of these controls and see that they are applied consistently. When employee misconduct is detected, decisive action must be taken, both to correct a problem that will otherwise continue and to send a signal to other employees. Such actions should result in decreases in theft and inefficiency by communicating to all employees the importance of honest and accurate work. Not only should the application of these controls have a beneficial effect on employee morale, but customers should be better served, and profits should increase.

NOTES

1. Joseph T. Wells, "Six Common Myths About Fraud," *Journal of Accountancy*, February 1990, p. 82.

2. Wanda A. Wallace, *Handbook of Internal Accounting Controls* (Englewood Cliffs, N.J.: Prentice-Hall, 1984).

3. Ibid.

4. Ibid., p. 45.

5. Neil H. Snyder, O. Whitfield Broome, Jr., and Karen Zimmerman, "Using Internal Controls to Reduce Employee Theft in Small Businesses," *Journal of Small Business Management*, July 1989, pp. 48–55.

6. Marvin Levy, *Detection of Errors, Fraud and Illegal Acts* (New York: AICPA, 1990); Marvin M. Levy, "Financial Fraud: Schemes and Indicia," *Journal of Ac-*

countancy, August 1985, pp. 78–87; Marshall J. Richter, "Shrinking the Embezzlement Loophole," *The Practical Accountant*, October 1985, pp. 67–70; Marshall J. Richter, "Fraud: The Accountant as Detective," *The National Public Accountant*, April 1984, pp. 18–23.

CHAPTER 8

Using Physical Security Devices to Reduce Employee Theft

As we have established previously, employee theft is an important concern for owners and managers of all types of businesses. Research indicates that all companies experience internal theft, and most employees will admit that they have stolen from their employers at some point in their careers. We have indicated that employee theft appears in many forms, whether tangible or intangible. The evidence is clear: Employee theft is a widespread problem that deserves high-level management attention and action.

With regard to physical shrinkage, most managers believe that employee theft is not a serious problem because most employees who steal take things that "don't amount to much." Thus the managers tend to ignore the problem. The evidence, however, suggests that this simply is not the case. We previously cited the U.S. Department of Commerce's estimate that employees steal about $40 billion annually from employers. To put this figure into perspective, $40 billion equals nearly 1.5 percent of all world trade.

With regard to time theft and theft of other intangibles, we have revealed the problem to have a price tag in excess of $200 billion a year. Intangible theft is virtually ignored, however, in most businesses.

The statistics are staggering. Insurance companies estimate that almost one-third of all business failures in the United States are due to employee theft, and others estimate that 50 percent of business failures may be

We thank A. Keene Byrd of Byrd Enterprises, Inc., in Charlottesville, Virginia, for his generous assistance in developing prices for the physical security devices discussed in this chapter.

due to theft. Managers who choose to overlook the theft problem or who accept it as a cost of doing business clearly may jeopardize the futures of their firms.

Several methods have been proposed for dealing with the employee theft problem. They include hiring people who are not likely to steal from the firm, establishing an organizational climate that does not support or condone theft, using appropriate internal controls, and prosecuting thieves once they are detected. Another method, and the one dealt with in this chapter, is the use of appropriate physical security devices.

The security industry offers a wide array of devices aimed at preventing theft. The simple locks and keys of the past have given way to sophisticated methods of access control and of perimeter and warehouse protection. This chapter examines some of the more frequently used physical security devices that are available today in an effort to assist business owners and managers who are coming to grips with the theft problem. It does not provide an in-depth treatment of any of them. To obtain additional information, expert assistance should be sought.

EMPLOYEE REACTIONS TO PHYSICAL SECURITY DEVICES

Before reviewing the security devices available, it is necessary to point out that employee reactions to increases in the level of security in their work environment may be negative. Increased attention to security may reduce the theft problem but, at the same time, alienate employees. Thus, as indicated previously, the benefits gained from theft control measures can be lost because of decreases in morale and productivity. Roy Carter, a recognized security expert, states that aggressive security will "render working conditions both inefficient and intolerable."[1] Leonard Sipes, another security expert, expresses a similar concern when he states that "traditional security interventions are necessary, but alone they cause resentment."[2] This point cannot be overemphasized. Employees will not react favorably if they think that "Big Brother" is constantly watching them, and they may begin to play games with management that could threaten the viability of the business itself. Furthermore, as more devices are introduced, some employees may try to find ways to outsmart management and circumvent the system.

To alleviate these problems, it is imperative to involve the employees themselves in developing the theft reduction program and to introduce the physical security devices as part of a comprehensive effort that addresses the litany of issues affecting employee theft (e.g., the work climate, hiring practices, and internal control procedures). Additionally, there must be acceptance by employees of what constitutes theft, and as we have repeatedly emphasized, management must set an example for employees by never engaging in activities that can be viewed as theft. This may require a change of attitude on the part of the owners and managers. Finally, the logic for the program must be clear, and the rewards for successful implementation of the program must be specific and must affect the employees directly.

GUARD SELECTION

Another issue that should be examined before discussing physical security devices is the process of selecting guards when, and if, they are needed. The role of the guard today is much more complex and difficult than it was just a few years ago, and any attempt to improve physical security without giving careful attention to the guards who monitor the system is doomed to failure. As security expert Vince Papi suggests, "today's guards often have to interface with high-tech security systems, know first aid and CPR, and act as company reps to greet people if they are placed in the lobby."[3] Belden Menkus lists eight questions that should be answered before choosing a commercial security service.

1. What wage rate is the company prepared to pay?
2. Where does the service primarily recruit for its security force?
3. Are security members expected to be fluent in English?
4. Does the service verify the suitability of the members of its force?
5. What kinds of routine training do security force members receive?
6. Does the service provide suitable uniforms for security force members?
7. Are security force members rotated periodically between work stations and shifts?
8. Does the service actively supervise individual security force members on the job?[4]

Once these questions have been answered satisfactorily, it is important for the company to clearly and succinctly explain its needs and concerns to the potential guard service. A breakdown in the guard selection process can negate the impact of any physical security device.

ACCESS CONTROLS

The use of access controls can be traced back to around 1000 B.C. when the Chinese developed a control system to guard their Imperial Palace.

Each member of the palace staff wore a ring engraved with intricate designs that identified which areas of the palace they were allowed to enter.[5]

Today access controls range from simple locks and keys to sophisticated systems that use biometrics. Access controls can help to reduce employee theft in a variety of ways. The most obvious uses include controlling admission to the workplace, parking lots, computer rooms, files, and office equipment. Not only can many of the systems monitor who enters a specific area, but they also can allow employees to enter only certain areas at certain times of the day. Furthermore, many access control systems incorporate the microprocessor and are therefore able to provide managers with an audit trail. Electronic access controls became quite popular during the 1980s. It was estimated that by 1990 this industry would reach total sales of more than $1.6 billion.[6]

Key Control Systems

The most basic of the access controls is the lock and key. One of the major problems with this method is key control. In medium-sized and large businesses it is nearly impossible for managers to know who is approved to use each key, what times they are allowed to use them, and the locations of all keys. Another drawback of the simple lock and key method is that it does not permit the recording of who entered each area, when they entered, and when they left.

Several methods have been introduced to alleviate some of the problems with key control. They include key cabinets, mass duplication, master keys, and electronic locks. Although these newer methods are improvements over the older key control technique and are much less expensive than some of the other access control systems, they all have serious problems.

The disadvantages of these methods are readily apparent. Key cabinets require constant monitoring to prevent misuse. Master key systems suffer from this problem as well, and in addition it is expensive to rekey every lock if the master key is lost or stolen. Electronic locks are the best of the methods introduced thus far. However, the codes on electronic locks must be changed often to prevent a security breakdown.[7]

The most advanced key control technology available involves the use of a computer. This system, although costly, alleviates most of the problems described above by requiring keys to be obtained from a wired panel that is linked to a computer. This linkage permits managers to identify employees who are allowed access to given areas. An employee who wants to use a key must complete a key request and input it into the computer. If the employee has been approved, the key is released from the panel.

This system allows managers to control access to certain areas; it helps to maintain accountability; it provides an audit trail; and it enables managers to make changes quickly, easily, and inexpensively.[8] It has disadvantages as well. Lock picking is always a possibility. Employees may loan the keys to others (although the existence of the audit trail should reduce this temptation). Also, loss of any key may necessitate changing the locks. Finally, if only a password is used by employees to gain access to the keys, it is possible for unauthorized employees to gain access to others' passwords.

The cost of key control systems varies widely, depending on the type of system chosen and the city in which the purchase is made. To reduce the cost of key control systems, owners and managers should select systems that satisfy their needs but do not exceed them.

Emergency Exits

Combining security and emergency exits is a common way to reduce employee theft. The security device is placed on exit doors and a sign is posted stating that use of the doors is for emergency purposes only. An alarm will sound whenever the door is opened. Additionally, concealed inside the door is a rod exit panel. When the door closes the astragal bar moves back into place and interlocks, thus preventing re-entry. The lock mechanism is not susceptible to picking.[9] This system is quite basic, however, and does not allow for the use of many of the advantages of the computer-based key control system. Nonetheless, the use of security doors is beneficial for back exits or other areas where high-level security is not required. The prices of emergency exits begin at about $300.

Magnetic Door Systems

A more advanced system incorporating magnetic doors also is available. A person attempting to use this type of door during a nonemergency is instructed to press a bar for several seconds. When the bar is pressed an alarm sounds and closed-circuit television is activated to monitor the situation. Another option available with magnetic doors is two-way communication between security personnel and the person attempting to use the exit. Taken together, these options make magnetic door systems effective in controlling access to sensitive areas. The prices of magnetic door systems begin at about $600.

Photo Identification Cards

Although photo identification (ID) cards are used widely today by many businesses, they are not very effective in controlling access. A manager who must rely on them exclusively may be opening the door to employee theft. The problems associated with these cards are particularly severe as the number of employees increases. At peak periods (i.e., 8:00 A.M. or during shift changes) it is virtually impossible for guards to examine every ID card even if they are displayed prominently. Thus the ID card is rendered ineffective at critical times during the day. Also, duplication of these cards is a relatively simple matter. Finally, systems that use photo ID cards exclusively are not capable of storing in memory the comings and goings of individuals. This shortcoming can be a significant drawback to the use of photo ID cards.

Photo IDs are relatively inexpensive. Prices begin at about $1 per card.

Access Control Cards

Access control cards have become extremely popular. The four cards most widely used today are magnetic stripe, magnetic dot, embedded wire, and passive proximity cards. Each of these technologies requires employees to insert their cards into a card reader. These readers may be located at various points where access control is desired. Moreover, all four types of cards are capable of handling thousands of employees and may use hundreds of access points.

Access control cards have several advantages over mechanical locks, key systems, and photo ID cards. They are easy to void if an employee should lose a card or leave the company. A lost key, or the loss of an employee who does not return a key, may necessitate purchasing new locks. Access control cards are much more difficult to duplicate than keys and ID cards. Additionally, they eliminate the use of locks, which are always prone to picking. The prices of access control systems vary, but the readers required to implement most of the systems available cost from $1,500 to $2,000.

Magnetic Stripe Cards

Magnetic stripe cards utilize a pattern of digital data that is recorded on a strip of magnetic material. A tape recorder–like head reads the cards as employees insert them through a slot in devices that are placed in strategic locations.[10] The magnetic stripe cards are the least expensive of the electronic cards available. They also are advantageous because they are capable of storing large amounts of data. Unfortunately they have several disadvantages that may reduce their overall attractiveness. High maintenance requirements have been reported with respect to the card-reader machines. The magnetic stripes also are susceptible to frequent abrasion. Moreover, counterfeiting, card slot vandalism, and data-reading errors are distinct possibilities.[11] The prices of magnetic stripe cards begin at about $1.50 each when purchased in quantity.

Magnetic Dot Systems

With magnetic dot systems, plastic sheets surround a magnetic material that is charged either positively or negatively. These cards are similar to the magnetic stripe cards in that employees insert them into slots on card readers. The magnetically coded areas of the card actuate a sensor in the reader. These cards also are relatively inexpensive, although not quite as economical as the magnetic stripe cards. They also are prone to vandalism and to durability problems associated with both the cards and the readers. Prices for magnetic dot systems begin at about $2.50 for each card.

Embedded Wire Cards

Embedded wire cards, also known as Weigand cards, use magnetic wires to generate a code number. The cards contain twenty-six to thirty-seven bits of data that a reader decodes when the card is passed through a sensing device. The advantage of embedded wire cards is their price. Additionally, they cannot be damaged easily. However, sometimes card wear and improper readings hamper this system. The prices of embedded wire cards begin at about $2.50 each, but the readers used with embedded wire cards cost only $200 to $400.

Passive Proximity Cards

Proximity cards are more expensive than the other three types of cards. They are made of a fiberglass-epoxy material and contain a group of passive tuned-circuits. When the card is held within a few inches of a sensing device, the pattern of resonant frequencies is read and relayed to a remote card reader for decoding. Durability is the major advantage of proximity cards. They are safe from the effects of weather, vandalism, and dirt. The prices of passive proximity cards range from $6 to $8 each without photos and from $7.50 to $9.50 each with photos.

The Keypad, or PINpad, System

The keypad, or PINpad, system can be used alone or in conjunction with other types of systems. In fact, a common method for increasing the level of security is to incorporate the keypad and card systems into one unit. The keypad resembles a telephone keypad, and works in one of two ways. The first method uses one number that is programmed into the computer. To gain access to a particular door, an employee must punch in the correct access code for that door. A second method assigns each employee a personal identification number (PIN). The number of authorized employees are entered into the computer memory, and after an authorized employee keys in his or her number, the door may be opened. Some employees object to carrying access cards. If this is the case, management would be wise to consider a keypad system. As discussed earlier, employee acceptance is important for any theft reduction program to be successful.

This system has drawbacks too. Employees can reveal their codes to their friends. In addition, this system increases through-time significantly. The more employees who must use this system and the more frequently they must use it, the more onerous the problem becomes. Employees often become angry when they have to wait in line.

Prices of this type of system begin at about $400. When used in conjunction with other systems, the price increases, but secondary verification is an idea worth considering. Using multiple systems can be extremely effective in reducing employee theft.

Voice-Activated Systems

Voice-activated systems can enroll up to 4,000 employees and do not require constant monitoring. Most employees are comfortable with voice-activated systems because they are accustomed to speaking into the telephone. Through-time is increased about three seconds for each person.[12] The prices of voice-activated systems begin at about $500.

Biometrics

The most recent innovations in access control involve biometrics. Biometrics can be used instead of cards and digital codes or in conjunction with these systems to provide a means of secondary verification. The systems also are successful in eliminating time theft. Biometrics use unique human characteristics such as fingerprints, retinal eye patterns, or signatures to verify the identity of the person attempting to gain access. Although these systems currently are expensive, the prices are expected to decline as technology becomes even more advanced.[13] Because the biometric systems take more time and are more expensive, they are recommended only at critical access points. Prices for biometric systems begin at about $800; they can cost a lot more.

Fingerprint Scanning

One company offers a fingerprint scanner that can be run on an IBM XT computer for $3,500. The scanner is able to match a fingerprint held in the air with one in its computer memory. Three fingers are included in the computer memory in case the person has a bandage or something similar on his or her finger. After punching in a correct access code, the employee holds his or her finger in the air. If, after two attempts, the fingerprints do not match, an alarm sounds for a guard.

Retinal Eye Pattern Scanner

The systems that use retinal eye patterns work in a similar manner. They match the eye's pattern of blood vessels with those entered in the computer. The employee must stand in front of the scanner as an infrared light source scans the eye at 320 points.[14] Once a match is made, access is immediately given. These systems cost about $6,000; but users claim that they pay for themselves in three months.[15]

Signature Verification

Signature verification has recently become more popular, especially in banks and other industries that use signatures more often. Two types of signature verification exist: static and dynamic. Dynamic is the better of the two because it analyzes how the person signs his name rather than what the final result looks like. For example, the way a "t" is crossed or how many times the pen is picked up and then pressed back to the paper are analyzed in a dynamic system. Again, the drawbacks to this system include increased through-time and expense.

PROTECTION OF ASSETS

Asset Tagging

In addition to controlling access to certain areas, on occasion it is important to control the company's assets that are located inside specific work stations or warehouses. There are several devices designed for this purpose. One involves the identification of assets by tagging. Several advances recently have been made in this area, and managers are now able to protect equipment and merchandise with a high degree of confidence. One major advancement is electronic article surveillance (EAS). This method involves tagging expensive equipment, such as tools and typewriters, with EAS devices that trigger an alarm when the articles are removed from their designated areas. Retail stores began using EAS in an effort to reduce shoplifting, and now other businesses have begun to take advantage of this technology to reduce employee theft. These systems cost $3,000 or more, and can be integrated with other systems through the use of microprocessors.

Bar Code Systems

Security managers have begun to use bar codes to protect the firm's assets from internal theft. Most people are familiar with these codes, since they are used widely in supermarkets.

In businesses that handle classified documents, bar codes can be imprinted directly on documents, and employees who want to copy them must use bar-coded identification cards to activate copying machines. An unsuccessful attempt by an employee to activate a copying machine will cause the computer with which the machine is networked to record the employee's number and the number of the document he or she was attempting to copy. This system is not foolproof, since the documents can be taken out of the building and copied on machines that are not part of the company's computer network.

Bar codes also can be used to keep track of tools and equipment that are taken from one location to another. If employees borrow them, the company's computer will have a record. In addition, bar codes are useful for scanning inventory. Periodic inventory checks using bar codes can be accomplished in a fraction of the time that it takes to conduct an inventory manually. The time required to take inventory can be reduced by as much as 90 percent when the bar code method is used.

The most important advantage of the bar code method is its price. The necessary equipment normally pays for itself during the first year of use,[16] and bar code systems are simple and easy to install. Another important advantage is accuracy. A typical bar code system averages one error per 3,379,000 characters. This accuracy rate is much better than the four keystroke errors per 1,000 entries made by a trained data entry clerk.[17] Because inventory can be taken more frequently, the information obtained is very accurate, and employees cannot easily tamper with inventory results, bar code systems have proved to be effective in helping to reduce employee theft.

Bar code systems cost $3,000 or more. They are gaining popularity because they are very accurate.

Lighting

Using appropriate lighting is one of the least expensive and most effective obstacles to would-be thieves. Increased lighting in areas that surround a warehouse will reduce employee theft and deter outside intruders. Employees are less likely to leave a piece of equipment or company inventory outside with the idea of taking it later if the area surrounding the building is well lighted. Likewise, employees who work until after dark are hesitant to leave work with things that do not belong to them if the parking lot is brightly lighted. The chart below compares the performance of selected light sources.[18]

Light Source	Average Illumination Performance
Incandescent	10–20 lumens* per watt
175-watt mercury vapor	70 lumens per watt
400-watt high-pressure sodium	125 lumens per watt
400-watt metal halide	85 lumens per watt
180-watt low-pressure sodium	180 lumens per watt

*Lumen is a technical term used to describe illumination levels. Lumens per watt is how much light is produced per watt of electricity required to operate the lamp.

Mercury vapor and high-pressure sodium lights are widely used today. Low-pressure sodium and metal halide lights are beneficial for more specialized lighting needs. Each of these light sources belongs to a family of light sources known as high-intensity discharge lamps (HIDs). They are more energy-efficient and provide significantly more illumination per watt than conventional incandescent lights. Using HIDs in strategic locations has proved to be effective in maintaining security and reducing theft. These lights also are available with photoelectric controls that enable them to be turned on and off automatically.

In addition to the type of lights available, other issues must be considered when developing an effective lighting system, for example the height of light poles and the distance between them. Additionally, the color of the buildings and parking lots being illuminated by the lights plays an important role in determining the optimum light source for a given situation.

Closed-Circuit Television

Closed-circuit television (CCTV) is a more sophisticated and expensive alternative to reduce employee theft. CCTV typically is used in areas where valuable and easily concealed assets are stored or handled. One important drawback with CCTV is that employees may view its use as an invasion of privacy and/or overkill. CCTV conjures up thoughs of "Big Brother" always watching, and its use can send a clear message that people are not trusted unless the need is apparent. If employees do not "buy in" to the use of CCTV, it is quite likely that productivity and morale will decline when the system is implemented. Thus firms considering CCTV would be well advised to be cautious and objective. The prices of CCTV systems begin at about $1,000.

PERIMETER PROTECTION

The discussion of perimeter protection is divided into two parts: outdoor perimeters and building perimeters. These two areas necessitate the use of different control devices. Perimeter protection system prices vary widely, depending on the type of system and the size and topography of the areas being protected.

Outdoor Perimeter Protection

The most basic outdoor perimeter protection is a standard chain link fence. Security can be increased through the use of barbed wire or razor wire wrapped around the top of a six- to eight-foot fence. Additional security can be provided by using fence-mounted disturbance sensors.

Sensors can detect any mechanical vibrations of the fence and trigger an alarm if someone tries to climb over or crawl under the fence. The most common types of sensors include electromechanical switches, piezoelectric transducers, geophones, and electric cables.[19] One of the advantages of these sensors is that they can be mounted directly on an existing fence and therefore follow the contours of the ground. One problem with the system is that an intruder is detected only if he comes in contact with the fence.

Electric-field sensors are another option for protecting perimeter fences. These sensors generate an electrostatic field in which motion can be detected. Intruders who enter the electric field trigger an alarm.

Invisible barrier detectors are another type of sensor device that can be used to increase security. They generate an invisible beam of electromagnetic energy, either infrared or microwave, that is distorted when someone walks or crawls through the beam. The use of invisible barrier detectors is not recommended if hills, gullies, or obstacles such as trees are present in the area that is to be protected.[20] It also is important to consider vegetation and climate in the area before purchasing a perimeter detector.

Building Perimeter Protection

Maintaining building perimeter security is important in reducing employee theft. For example, unprotected openings covered by glass, such as windows and skylights, provide abundant opportunities for would-be thieves. Inexpensive lead foil strips can be applied to the glass, and if the glass is broken, an alarm is triggered. There are two problems with lead foil strips. First, they are unattractive. Second, they can be broken fairly easily under normal working conditions. Alternatives to lead foil strips include piezoelectric detectors and mercury-filled switches. Both of these devices require the addition of an attachment to each windowpane. This alternative would be expensive if a large number of windows needed protection.

More sophisticated and attractive devices can be used to detect glass breakage. For example, audio discriminators can detect the sound of breaking glass. The audio discriminator cannot be used in areas where there is much activity, however, because excessive or random noises will activate the alarm. Shock sensors suffer from the same problem. These sensors react to shock waves that are emitted during glass breakage.

Microwave, ultrasonic, and infrared sensors can be used for theft reduction. Microwave and ultrasonic devices are extremely sensitive. This may be an advantage or a disadvantage. The more sensitive the device, the higher the level of protection. However, the more sensitive the device, the more likely you will encounter false alarms. Both of these sensors have another, more serious drawback: They can be used only where the temperature ranges between 20 and 120 degrees Fahrenheit.[21] Passive infrared sensors are not obstructed by temperature extremes, but they fail to detect the presence of someone who is hiding behind an obstacle in the room. Using a ceiling-mounted infrared unit will help to alleviate this problem.

Unfortunately creative employees who are willing to assume a small degree of risk can beat these systems. Thus they are frequently used simultaneously and in conjunction with other security devices.

CONCLUSION

Physical security devices can be effective in reducing employee theft. The sophistication of the systems available varies widely, as do the prices of the systems. There is a system on the market for almost any need, and owners and managers should consider how, and if, their particular circumstances could be improved by using appropriate physical security devices.

NOTES

1. Roy Carter, "Employee Theft Often Appears Legitimate," *Accountancy*, July 1987, p. 75.

2. Leonard A. Sipes, "Tradition Takes a Twist," *Security Management*, 31 (June 1987), p. 44.

3. Robert D. Franceschini, "Security: A Look at the Major Trends Buyers Should Know About," *Purchasing*, March 1987, p. 49.

4. Belden Menkus, "Eight Things to Know When Looking for a Commercial Security Service," *Administrative Management*, November 1986, p. 60.

5. Stuart Knott, "The ABCs of Access Control," *Security Management*, May 1987, p. 84.

6. Kellyn S. Betts, "Electronic Access Control Always Alert," *Modern Office Technology*, June 1986, p. 110.

7. George Blackstone, "Computerize Your Key Control," *Security Management*, October 1986, p. 48.

8. Ibid.

9. John Naudts, "Focus on Access Control," *Buildings*, April 1987, p. 86.

10. Knott, "The ABCs of Access Control," p. 85.

11. Naudts, "Focus on Access Control," p. 88.

12. "Proactive Strategies Prevent Office Crime," *Modern Office Technology*, October 1987, p. 109.

13. Abbey Brown, "Trends in the Security Industry," *Personnel Administrator*, May 1986, p. 53.

14. "Corporate Security Update '86," *Dun's Business Month Focus*, September 1986, p. 66.

15. Brown, "Trends in the Security Industry," p. 53.

16. David Grand, "Technology at Its Simplest," *Security Management*, March 1987, p. 33.

17. Ibid.

18. Neal Johnson, "Bright Spots in Security Planning," *Security Management*, October 1986, p. 64.

19. Clay E. Higgins, "Site Specific Perimeter Protection," *Security Management*, February 1986, p. 48.

20. Ibid.

21. Joseph A. Barry, "The World of Indoor Space, Part 1," *Security Management*, June 1987, p. 72.

CHAPTER 9

Reducing Time Theft

In previous chapters we have fully established that employee theft is a problem of great magnitude and appears in many forms. For example, employees may take tangible property such as cash and inventory, or they may steal intangible assets such as the time that their employers purchase from them for an agreed-upon price (i.e., salary and wages). It has been estimated that each year employees "steal" in excess of $175 billion worth of time for which they are paid by their employers in addition to the theft of tangible property.[1]

Although the theft of tangible property is the most obvious and most controllable form of employee theft, time theft is equally as pervasive throughout American businesses as more recognizable forms of theft. Simply by its nature, this form of theft is extremely difficult to detect and solve. One of the primary reasons for this difficulty is the attitude of most business owners and managers that time theft is a cost of doing business. As a result, the problem is ignored until it becomes so severe that it must be addressed. Even defining time theft is difficult, since most employees resent the suggestion that they "steal" time. And finally, the distinction between time theft, time waste, and normal behavior often is blurred and leads to much confusion among both employers and their employees.

What kind of behavior does constitute time theft, and how does this behavior impact your business? One recent study considered all personal activity engaged in while on the job as theft. As a result, the study determined that the typical employee "steals" six work weeks worth of time each year.[2] Is this a valid estimate? Can you reasonably expect your employees never to take personal time on the job?

A study conducted by Robert Half International identified the following as the most common forms of time theft:

- Habitual late arrival and/or early departure
- Feigned illnesses that lead to the taking of unwarranted sick days
- The use of company time to operate another business
- Inordinately long lunch hours and coffee breaks
- Constant socializing with other employees
- Excessive personal telephone calling
- Creating the need for overtime by slowing down production during normal hours[3]

The results of the study reveal the breadth of activities that some people call time theft. Consider, however, that instead of being deliberately dishonest, this type of behavior is more a reflection of other factors, including poor management strategy and lack of employee training. If so, these activities are not theft, but nothing more than time wasted.

Regarding personal time taken on the job, is it fair to say that not every instance of personal activity should be considered theft or time wasted? In fact, are there not many times when personal activity is entirely legitimate. For example, calling a child's doctor while at work to make an appointment is personal business but certainly does not qualify as time theft. Likewise, taking a two-hour lunch after the completion of a major job is therapeutic and likely to promote further productivity. Such behavior should not be considered time theft or time wasted, but time well spent.

Despite the obvious exceptions, most of the activities considered as time theft are clearly inappropriate and create a serious problem that must be addressed. However, dealing with the issue is complicated. Even though most time theft activities are inappropriate, unacceptable, and contrary to company policy, they seldom constitute actual theft. Instead, they represent time wasted. As one business owner suggested, this kind of behavior "is embedded in the fabric of our society."[4]

Clearly, time waste is a substantial problem that deserves attention. Business owners and managers have an obligation to identify activities that involve wasted time and to find constructive alternatives to reduce this inefficiency. The primary purpose of this chapter is to address the time waste issue and offer solutions to the problem.

ARE THEY PROBLEM EMPLOYEES OR EMPLOYEES WITH PROBLEMS?

To be sure, there are problem employees who will take advantage of any situation and steal time. Managers must be on their guard constantly to find them and deal with them before they engage in too much mischief. However, business people, who are active and under a lot of pressure, must be careful not to assume that all employees are prone to larceny and time theft. Frustration and lack of patience with people is common and understandable but should not lead to the conclusion that most employees are deliberately dishonest. In fact, most of them are honest but simply unaware that their behavior is inappropriate.

Consider, for instance, the example of a secretary in a large law firm. This person, by nature, is anxious to do a good job and willing to work hard when necessary. However, she has a tendency to arrive late, take frequent breaks, and spend much of the day talking to friends on the phone while typing documents. As a result, she not only has an abbreviated day within which to accomplish her work, but she also makes careless mistakes that require correction. Furthermore, she does not work as quickly as she can when fully concentrating on her task at hand and must work overtime to meet mandatory deadlines. Thus she imposes unnecessary costs on her firm.

This type of person usually enters the business world with bad work habits and does not view her behavior as inappropriate. In all likelihood no one has ever criticized her lack of productivity during regular business hours because she always has managed to get her work done by the assigned deadline. In fact, her willingness to work overtime is probably viewed positively, and she may get "brownie points" for her willingness to do it. It is a sad commentary, but most business owners and managers will accept any approach that results in successful completion of a task, no matter how inefficient it is. Again, it is simply accepted as a cost of doing business.

Thus, instead of being inveterate thieves, employees merely behave at work as they have all of their lives. They bring with them to the job a host of problems and bad habits that cause them to act in an unprofessional, unproductive, and often unacceptable manner. For example, most employees have the following characteristics:

- A tendency to procrastinate
- Poorly developed management skills
- A poor understanding of the importance of goals and objectives
- Poorly defined priorities
- A tendency to operate in the crisis management mode

- A tendency to be involved in too many activities
- A tendency to equate activity and productivity

Few people enter a job situation with the planning, organizing, and scheduling skills or the self-discipline that is essential for effective and efficient job performance. Thus they waste time. But, again, to interpret their actions as theft is incorrect in most instances, and it may lead to the implementation of inappropriate solutions.

FINDING THE SOLUTION

If an employee is consciously and deliberately abusing the freedom provided by the organization and "stealing" time, then the solution should be obvious. That person should be dismissed. For instance, had the same secretary previously mentioned continued to evince nonproductive work habits, after being confronted with her lack of productivity and given the opportunity to improve her basic skills, she should have been terminated. To do otherwise would send a signal to everyone that time theft is acceptable and could lead other employees to emulate the bad work habits of offenders. It eventually could result in a reduction of productivity, profitability, and morale.

Most employees are not deliberate thieves. They simply do not understand the significance of their actions or are unaware that their work habits are problematic. As a result, they simply waste time. The appropriate solution for these employees would be to design programs and activities to improve their performance. Below are several suggestions that will help to reduce time waste in organizations.

Focus on the Attitudes of Employees and Managers

According to Snyder and Blair, "Theft is a state of mind—nothing more. Prevention and control are merely states of awareness and caring. Physical security cannot solve the problem because the physical acts do not constitute the problem: the mental attitude behind them does."[5] Therefore, managers must attack the problem by focusing their attention on its root cause: employee attitudes. Changing employee attitudes is the key to solving the problem.

Take, for example, our secretary, who seemingly is unaware of the significance of her behavior. She is nonproductive during the day, has to work overtime as a result, and uses rationalization for justification. If everyone else does it and gets paid for it, why not? In this situation the employee's attitude clearly is inappropriate; however, theft has not occurred. It is management's obligation to enumerate for the employee what is acceptable behavior and what is not before there is any hope of improvement. Managers must take an active stand in changing and redirecting employees' attitudes.

Thus passive acceptance, whether related to physical shrinkage or to wasted time, is nonproductive. If managers assume that their employees will waste time regardless of the actions they take, and make no positive steps toward dealing with the problem, then they are defeated before they start. Managers must adopt the attitude that time waste can be reduced significantly and then act accordingly.

Send a Clear Message to All Employees

A clear signal that time waste can, and will, be reduced must be sent to all employees. The way in which this is done is crucial. To produce the desired result, the issue must be presented in a compelling manner. For example, employees might be asked to participate in a program to increase productivity rather than a program to reduce wasted time. The former has positive connotations and the latter, negative. Employees are much more likely to respond to the problem and support a solution if the issue is presented in a positive manner.

Before any productivity program can be successful, managers must be willing to practice what they preach. If our legal secretary's supervising attorney spends an inordinate amount of time making nonbusiness-related calls, takes long lunches, and pads his time sheets to make up for lost billable hours, how can he expect her to perform in an honest and productive manner? Therefore, it is imperative that managers demonstrate their support for a productivity program by manifesting the same work habits and values that they expect their employees to adopt. Without setting an example, managers' efforts to improve productivity often will be futile.

Foster Morale and Open the Lines of Communication

Paying attention to employee morale and making certain that the lines of communication are always open have positive effects on productivity. Although good morale is no guarantee that employees will be productive, poor morale almost always results in lost productivity. In an environment characterized by low morale, employees spend a great deal of time talking and worrying about their working conditions instead of doing their jobs.

Fortunately morale is a variable over which managers can exert significant influence by their actions. Care should be taken by managers, therefore, to make certain that they act in a manner that is likely to produce the desired results. Probably the most important actions they can take to improve employee morale are to open the lines of communication with employees, to listen to them, and to use their suggestions to make any required changes. In doing so employees are made to feel like part of the team and learn that their input is valued. And once they have "joined the team," employees are likely to become powerful forces in helping to increase productivity.

Delegate Responsibility to Employees

Employees have the capacity to accomplish much more than many managers expect from them. Delegation of responsibility to employees is a way of tapping this underutilized resource. Additionally, employees have the potential to become effective monitors of one another's performance and can lessen the need for managers to play the role of policemen. When given more responsibility and control, employees will feel more independent and, as a result, their attitudes will improve.

Ideally, abusers of the system should be detected by their peers who are unhappy with their behavior and unwilling to accept it.[6] When employees play this role effectively, managers can expect productivity to increase. As a result, managers can devote more of their time and attention to the many important issues that tend to be ignored or given only scant attention under normal conditions in most businesses.

Measure the Results of the Program and Promote Productivity Improvement

The ability to measure the results of the program is crucial to its success for two reasons. First, simply having a productivity improvement program in place could become mere window dressing unless there is tangible evidence that something meaningful is being accomplished. Second, employees need and want to track their individual progress in improving productivity. Therefore, although actual time waste is difficult to quantify, measuring and recording productivity are relatively straightforward and can provide valuable tools to managers.

And if these measured results ever consistently fall below expectation, managers can help by identifying new and innovative ways to accomplish these goals. In doing so they can revitalize employee attitudes and promote improved productivity.

Set Goals and Hold Managers Accountable for Producing Results

Specific productivity improvement goals should be set with the participation of the employees who are actually doing the work. Their involvement in the goal-setting process is critical to the program's success, and their ability to achieve the goals should play an important part in their individual success. After these goals are established, managers must be held responsible and accountable for producing results. Just as a manager's subordinates should be evaluated on the basis of productivity, so should the manager be evaluated on his ability to promote this productivity among his employees.

Finally, the program must be designed in such a way that tangible rewards accrue to the employees and the managers who are involved in its success. To adapt an adage, "if the people are not rewarded for achieving the goals, then they will not achieve them."

Develop and Implement a Training Program to Reinforce Values

Training is required to help employees develop the skills they need to improve their productivity. The obvious skills they need, and the ones that get the most attention, are the technical skills that are directly related to job performance. Other skills that are only indirectly related to job performance, such as planning, organizing, scheduling, delegating, and communicating, are at least as important as the technical skills. Yet these skills get much less attention. The ability to deal with personal problems such as bad work habits and poor self-discipline is virtually ignored in most training programs. Problems in these areas, however, often underlie problems existing in the technical areas.

Therefore, an effective training program should address all of the skills listed above, beginning immediately after hire and continuing throughout an employee's career. In the early years of employment, training should focus on the more basic skills. In the later years more advanced and specialized skills are needed. Additionally, training should provide regular reinforcement opportunities to prevent bad habits from resurfacing.

Provide Regular Review and Feedback

Finally, regular evaluation and feedback are imperative. Managers should review their employees' performance regularly to provide them with the feedback they need to know how well they are progressing. Managers also should use these sessions to explore any problems or difficulties employees are experiencing and to solicit input on ways to improve productivity.

CONCLUSION

Although time theft has received a great deal of attention recently, what most people call time theft is not theft at all. In reality, most employees enter the work situation with bad habits and poor job skills that cause them to act in inappropriate and unacceptable ways that waste valuable time. Dealing with the problem requires managers to focus their attention on the employee attitudes that create the problem and on a willingness to adjust their own behavior and managerial strategy accordingly.

Programs to reduce time waste should be designed and presented as programs to improve productivity. The latter approach has positive connotations and provides opportunities to involve employees directly in efforts that can produce tangible results for the firm and for them personally. Thus setting specific improvement goals, tracking employee performance, and rewarding employee achievements are critical to the success of a productivity improvement program.

Additionally, opening the lines of communication between managers and employees is essential for the successful implementation of such a program. Doing so enables managers to focus attention on the values and work ethic that lead to increased levels of productivity and to influence the issues that directly affect employee morale.

Finally, training programs should be developed and implemented simultaneously with the productivity improvement program to increase the likelihood of success and to reinforce the values that lead to improved job performance.

NOTES

1. James Walls, "Preventing Employee Theft," *Management Review*, September 1985, pp. 48–50.
2. James B. Moore, "Stolen Time Plagues Employers," *The Journal*, Jan. 12, 1987, p. A10.
3. Harry Bacas, "Stealing Time: The Subtlest Theft," *Nation's Business*, June 1987, p. 23.
4. Roger Weinheimer, business executive, personal interview.
5. Neil H. Snyder and Karen Blair, "Dealing with Employee Theft," *Business Horizons*, May-June 1989, p. 5.
6. Leonard Sandridge, vice president for finance, University of Virginia, personal interview.

CHAPTER 10

Conclusion

Employee theft is one of the most serious problems facing businesses in the United States today. Reliable estimates suggest that about one-third of all business failures can be directly attributed to employee theft and that employees steal more than $40 billion annually from their employers—that is ten times the cost of street crime in America. In addition, the problem is escalating at a 15 percent annual rate.

We have shown in this book that employee theft is a complex problem. It involves management issues at the strategic and operational levels and ethical and legal questions. Despite its obvious complexity, employee theft is a people problem, and it must be dealt with like other important people problems. First and foremost, the owners and managers of a business must recognize that the problem exists, and they must take steps to solve it.

The solution to the problem begins at the top of any business. It emanates from upper management and filters down through each and every employment level. As we have emphasized again and again, owners and managers set the example that others will follow. Like Caesar's wife, they must be beyond reproach. To obtain and maintain a high level of employee honesty, integrity, and motivation, owners and managers must demonstrate these qualities themselves.

Firms that experience significant employee theft have learned that it is like a cancer; it gets worse over time unless owners and managers take the initiative and develop a strategy to reduce it. Owners and top managers must accept their responsibility and demonstrate their commitment to a theft reduction program if it is to have any chance of working. They must create conditions in their firms that will not support thieves and will choke them out of the business. In other words, owners and managers must make working for their business so unattractive to thieves that they will not want to stay.

Unfortunately most owners and managers avoid dealing with employee theft because it is an unpleasant task and because they think they can safely ignore it. During good times it is possible to overlook the problem without experiencing undue risks because margins are high enough to support theft. Although high margins reduce the urgency of solving the problem, they allow lax management practices to develop and increase the likelihood of even more employee theft in the future. When times are bad, lax management practices, slim margins, and attitudes that suggest theft is acceptable combine to destroy many businesses and seriously weaken many others.

Another reason owners and managers prefer not to deal with employee theft is that there is no simple definition of theft. Business owners possess a wide range of values and beliefs, and so do their employees. They all see the world differently, and they define theft differently. Therefore, actions that are viewed as theft in one business may not be viewed as theft in another. But most business owners naively assume that their employees see things the way they do, and this assumption leads to much larceny.

To make matters worse, otherwise honest people will steal from their employers and believe sincerely that they are doing nothing wrong. For example, when employees believe that they are not being rewarded properly for their work, some of them will "steal." But in their opinions they are not stealing. They are merely getting what they deserve. Other employees might retaliate against their employers when they are angry by "stealing." But in their minds they are not stealing either. They are only getting even. Each of these examples represents theft by employees, but they are not examples of theft by people who are bona fide thieves.

No matter why it happens, theft affects attitudes and morale in businesses negatively. When a business has theft problems most of its employees know about it, and the honest ones do not like it. They would prefer not to work with thieves, and they resent the fact that owners and managers are not dealing with the problem. When this happens honest employees will either assume that the owners and managers of the business know about the problem and do not care, or that they do not know about it and are incompetent. Many of them will just quit, but others (the less honest ones) will do as their fellow employees are doing—steal.

There is another good reason to deal with the employee theft problem. In the preface to this book we said that the dollars saved by a theft reduction program are dollars that can be used to improve and modernize the business and to make the business more competitive. Stated another way, they are like an interest-free loan that never has to be repaid. The funds are already available. You simply need to re-evaluate your management strategies and business practices and then develop and implement a theft reduction program to gain access to them. This approach may sound simple, but in reality many complex and difficult questions have to be asked and answered before the problem is solved. This book has addressed most of them.

If you never lose sight of your goal to create an organization that will not attract or support thieves, your efforts will be well rewarded. By creating and maintaining an environment that provides solid ethics, well-outlined goals, effective communication, and sufficient controls, thieves will not want to work for you. The reputation of your organization as one that does not tolerate employee theft will allow you to reap many rewards. Dishonest employees will stay away, and advise their dishonest friends to do so as well. The risk for them in working for you will be simply too high. On the other hand, good employees will want to work for you, and they will be more likely to stay with your organization because you do not ignore dishonesty. To them, the message is clear—you care about your business and your employees.

As outlined in the previous chapters, an effective theft reduction program takes into account every aspect of your business. Each level, department, and region is important and should be addressed. They must work together consistently and in harmony to solve the problem. The approach to the problem described in this book will help you to identify your problem areas, to develop an effective solution, and ultimately to increase your profits considerably.

How to Hire and Keep Quality Employees

Ryan A. Kuhn

Among the most difficult tasks facing American business today is finding, hiring, and keeping quality employees.

As problems of poor productivity and internal theft grow, managers are increasingly finding their ability to obtain information on job applicants under attack by social legislation. At the same time, they are increasingly being held liable for the counterproductive or criminal acts of their employees.

How can you, as an employer, establish a proper balance between respect for the rights of job applicants and employees, and responsibility to protect company assets and personnel by conducting thorough, effective screening procedures?

Finding quality workers is made even tougher today by two trends that show no signs of reversing soon: (1) the baby boom is over and entry-level applicants are becoming scarce; (2) the American unemployment rate is extraordinarily low, in some places under 2 percent. Many individuals who remain unemployed under these circumstances are not desirable workers.

Aggressive and imaginative recruiting can help ease some of this labor shortage. For instance, unconventional sources of labor are senior citizens, recent immigrants, housewives, the disabled, and participants in government placement programs.

But the most dramatic relief from the labor crunch is realized by those employers who enjoy low turnover and high productivity. They achieve

Copyright © 1988 Reid Psychological Systems. Second edition. Reprinted with permission of the copyright holder.

these hallmarks of performance by carefully selecting their employees, by openly disciplining deviant behavior, and by undertaking specific steps that encourage worker satisfaction and commitment.

This appendix describes how you can choose the right job applicant–screening techniques for your business. And it sets out some simple rules that will, if you follow them, enable your business to maximize employee contribution and retain productive workers.

WHY SHOULD I CARE ABOUT HIRING QUALITY EMPLOYEES?

The Importance of Integrity

A key expression of employee quality is integrity on the job. Each year American workers steal about $50 billion in money and goods from their employers, according to recent U.S. Department of Justice figures, and this loss is increasing at the rate of 15 percent annually. Estimates of how much retailer shrink is due to employees range from 40 percent to 75 percent of the total. Still studies show that only 20 percent of all such insider theft is detected. By its nature, theft is a secret act. One reason so much insider theft goes unnoticed is that many managers don't realize the extent of the problem. Honest people typically don't believe that theft by employees is widespread. After all, *they* don't commit such acts—why should others? In fact, almost half of all employees at some time steal to some degree: everything from minor items like office supplies to major pieces of equipment like computers or air conditioners.

Thus the potential for dishonesty is a decisive factor in choosing which applicant should be hired for a job, especially if the job is lightly supervised and provides access to cash or valuable merchandise. Such environments increase the temptation for people who are prone to misconduct.

Ironically, research also indicates that theft-prone people are *attracted* to jobs that offer greater theft opportunity. In other words, where your company is most vulnerable is precisely where you will find the greatest concentration of dishonest applicants and employees.

Although employee theft of tangible items may cost billions, it pales in comparison to the money lost in theft of time. Employee "time theft"—excess breaks, long lunches, late arrivals, early departures, bogus sick days, deliberate slowness, and excessive socializing on the job—costs American employers as much as $170 billion annually.

Stolen time can add up quickly. Weekly losses per average time thief are about four and one-half hours. To put this number in perspective, the time wasted by these people consumes six work-weeks each year.

Research further shows that employees prone to steal time are far more likely to steal tangible items as well.

In fact, researchers have found that people who demonstrate attitudes commonly associated with on-the-job integrity also have lower levels of turnover, are less likely to file worker's compensation claims, are more likely to earn raises and promotions, experience lower shrink or theft losses among their subordinates, are more committed to the work ethic, and are more likely to be psychologically healthy.

The Costs of Drug Abuse

Substance abuse at work has recently gained recognition as a widespread and serious problem. Statistics compiled by the National Institute on Drug Abuse indicate that *44 percent of people entering the work force for the first time have used illegal drugs within the past year. Between 10 and 23 percent of all American workers used drugs on the job last year.*

Experts estimate that the use of drugs on the job costs American industry about $85 billion a year in lost productivity, and that drug and alcohol treatment accounts for 20 percent of employer-paid health insurance costs.

The cost of all forms of employee dishonesty—substance abuse, tangible theft, lost time, and related legal entanglements—total more than $300 billion each year. But even this massive figure doesn't include other costs directly related to such counterproductive actions. This behavior also degrades overall productivity by sapping others' morale, distracting productive workers, and heightening turnover, driving away those who don't want to associate with it.

How Legal Trends Are Affecting Employer Responsibilities

Rising litigation makes finding honest, reliable employees increasingly important. At stake is more than company assets and productivity: Businesses are being successfully sued by customers and workers for the crimes of their own employees, especially if it can be shown that the company did not apply rigorous job screening techniques. Employers are actually being held liable for having *too little* information about employees, a legal charge called "negligent hiring."

Negligent hiring charges typically are brought against a business by someone who is harmed by a working employee. The injured party may be another employee, a customer, or a member of the public. In such cases the person bringing suit claims that the business failed to use reasonable care in selecting its workers, thereby exposing others to risk.

The trend of recent court decisions imposes an affirmative duty on business to investigate carefully the background and psychological profile of those it hires.

Example: When the owner of an apartment complex hired a resident manager, he was unaware that his new employee had a history of convictions for violent crime. The manager later raped a tenant, who then successfully sued the owner for negligent hiring. The court ruled that the owner had a duty to exercise reasonable care in hiring people who could, as a result of their employment, pose a threat to members of the public.

The lengths to which an employer should go in checking an applicant's background depend, in part, on the position being filled. In this case it may have been difficult or expensive to complete a background check—yet the price for *not* checking was even greater.

Example: A Florida suit was brought by a woman whose husband, a bank guard, was killed by a fellow bank guard who became insane while on duty. The bank had checked references supplied by the criminal guard when he applied for work, and they seemed acceptable. The dead guard's widow sued for negligent hiring and won a $300,000 settlement. The court stated that the bank should not have relied solely on references supplied by the criminal guard himself, but should have conducted a thorough background check (even though such a check would have revealed no prior criminal behavior) and psychological tests. Such elaborate screening procedures were warranted because of the trust placed in the bank guard's job.

Another legal risk increasingly faced by employers is the "vicarious liability" suit, which holds a business responsible for the wrongful acts of employees perpetrated in the course of their duties. An example of this would be the security guard who apprehends a suspect on warehouse premises and then uses excessive force to subdue him. The suspect subsequently sues the guard's employer for his injuries, claiming vicarious liability.

The use of thorough pre-employment screening techniques, particularly psychological tests, can significantly reduce the employer's exposure to negligent hiring, vicarious liability, negligent supervision, and other charges.

(Another new legal issue that companies face is the recently imposed Immigration Control Act: Employers must fill out Form I–9 for each new hire, and are responsible for certifying job applicants' citizenship status. This act also makes it unlawful to discriminate against job applicants who look or sound like their country of origin might be other than the United States.)

The drug-using employee is a magnet for negligent hiring and vicarious liability suits as well as for other costs, such as the following:

- **Negligent supervision liability.** *Example:* A supervisor escorts an intoxicated employee to his car and allows him to drive home. The employee subsequently injures others in an accident.
- **Increased worker's compensation.** *Example:* An employee successfully claims that on-the-job stress has aggravated his drug dependency or caused his addiction.
- **Adverse publicity.** *Example:* Employee drug use demoralizes the drug-free work force and attracts unwelcome outside attention.
- **Increased insurance premiums.**

To reduce these growing threats, you need modern, accurate, and thorough screening procedures to identify and hire the best people available.

EFFECTIVE SCREENING TECHNIQUES

When you consider an employee for a sensitive, unsupervised assignment, you must determine the person's integrity and productivity based on reliable and nondiscriminatory evidence. Fact-based evidence—not intuition or general feelings about an employee—reduces or eliminates the risk of lawsuits and makes for objective, fair decisions. A description of a number of the most commonly used and effective screening techniques follows.

Application Forms and Resumés

To create needed documentation and to standardize an easy-to-read format for candidate histories, you need an application form. The form should include only questions that relate to the job and that are legal. Check the form carefully for completeness when handed in and then have it signed as a testament of its truthfulness in your presence. It also should include an admonishment about falsification (e.g., false statements are grounds for termination after hire) and a disclaimer regarding your inquiries (e.g., applicant won't be rejected on the basis of age, race, or religion).

Resumés provide crucial information about an applicant's work experience and educational history, but also are notorious for their inaccuracy: Research indicates that 30 percent of applicants' resumés contain material misrepresentations. To assure yourself that salary and education data supplied on resumés are accurate, ask applicants to provide you with copies of school transcripts and recent W–2 forms. This also cuts down on the time spent checking references.

Interviews

Trained interviewers, expert in the use of "structured interview" techniques, can be quite effective in evaluating responses to job-related questions. Such interviewers also are skilled in obtaining admissions of prior dishonest acts by assisting the interviewee in creating a rationale for the acts.

Unfortunately interviews conducted by untrained managers can be subjective, allowing for biased decisions. For example, the interviewer may be overly influenced by a single trait that affects his judgment of the applicant's overall suitability. Stereotyping is another problem: An applicant may be judged on group membership, such as race, instead of on relevant characteristics. And with the "similar-to-me" phenomenon, the interviewer judges an applicant by comparing the applicant's attitudes and values with the interviewer's own. This approach consistently produces discriminatory results.

To conduct interviews that are valid and free of such adverse impact, make sure your interview questions are closely linked to an analysis of the job being filled and criteria for performing it well. Schedule two interviews, with a different interviewer for each, and then compare notes. Structured interview guides and training also improve interviewer reliability and reduce bias.

Before you interview, keep these simple goals in mind:

- Obtain enough information to be able to determine whether the applicant will perform well on the job. Use a checklist.
- Give enough information to the applicant regarding the job, compensation, working conditions, and company policies and programs so he can decide whether he should accept it. Use a checklist.
- Establish a favorable attitude toward the job in the applicant's mind.

Here are some additional practical suggestions:

- Put the applicant at ease in an informal setting.
- Don't allow any interruptions.
- Don't rush.
- Ascertain the applicant's long-range goals to determine whether he is sufficiently motivated.

The following are interview or application form subjects that can be legally and openly discussed:

- Work history (including gaps)
- Circumstances of all previous employment, including reasons for leaving
- Skill levels required for position
- Applicant's legal right to work in United States.
- Previous criminal record, if any (except in New York State)
- Health and accidents that may impair job performance
- Willingness to take a physical examination if required for the job
- Factors that motivate the applicant to excel
- School grades

The following interview topics are restricted, prohibited, or suspect areas of inquiry:

- Age (even directly), except for "under 18"
- Place of birth
- History of unemployment and/or worker's compensation claims
- Life insurance; credit rating
- Arrest record
- Disabilities unrelated to the job under consideration
- Marital and family status; child-care arrangements
- National origin
- Race or color

The sample interview questions (See Table A.1), show how the subtle phrasing of an interview or application form question can make it acceptable or unacceptable.

The following are suggestions that encourage an applicant to respond freely during an interview and that improve two-way communication:

- Ask broad questions, ones that can't be answered with a simple yes or no, to determine the applicant's verbal ability. Require the applicant to select, organize, and present answers to you by asking questions like, "How did you happen to get interested in this field?"
- Ask your question and then stop talking.
- Ask the applicant to describe the sorts of tasks and problems encountered in previous jobs and then ask how the applicant solved these challenges.
- Avoid becoming so preoccupied with the next question that you

Table A.1
Sample Interview Questions

ACCEPTABLE	UNACCEPTABLE
Citizenship	
What language(s) do you speak and write fluently?	What is your native language?
Are you a citizen of the United States?	Of what country are you a citizen?
If you are not, do you have the legal right to remain permanently in the the United States?	
Financial Status	
Do you have reliable transportation to and from work?	Do you own a car?
	Do you have a valid driver's license (unless position requires driving)?
Can you supply a phone number by which you can be reached?	Do you have a telephone?
	Have your wages ever been garnisheed?
	Have you ever filed for bankruptcy?
	Have you ever been refused credit?
Religion	
Which days will you be available for work?	Which religious holidays do you observe?
	Do you have any religious objections to paying union dues?
Relatives	
Please supply the names of your relatives already employed by our company.	Please supply the names, addresses, ages, telephone numbers (or other information) concerning your spouse, children and relatives.
Physical Health	
Have you ever used illegal drugs? (Unacceptable in New York state.)	Have you ever filed a worker's compensation claim?
Number of days missed from work in the last year. (Don't count vacations.)	How many days leave have you taken off sick in the last year?
Do you have any ailments that might interfere with performing the job for which you are applying? If so, describe.	Please supply any physical ailments you have, the date of their occurrence, and their treatment.

don't hear the applicant's answers. Pay attention to the logical flow of the applicant's answers.

- If you meet with any inconsistencies, have the applicant reconcile them before concluding the interview.
- Be alert to vague answers that may be efforts by the applicant to cover up something.
- Before concluding, tell the applicant what the next step in your hiring procedure will be.

As soon as the interview is over, try to answer for yourself the following questions while the session is fresh in your mind:

Does the applicant have . . .

- The ability to do the job?
- The motivation to do an excellent job?
- A willingness to assume responsibility?
- A personality that lends itself to the atmosphere and image of the workplace?
- Initiative?
- Creativity (if relevant)?
- Loyalty (as evidenced by a history of commitment to prior jobs)?
- Perseverance?
- A desire to cooperate?
- Self-reliance (or will the applicant depend on other employees to get the job done)?
- Emotional maturity?
- Good abilities of self-expression?
- Good moral standards?

Score the applicant on each of these characteristics related to the requirements of the job, say, on a scale of 1 to 10. Then total the scores to compare an applicant's interview results with others. You'll find a sample post-interview evaluation on page 152.

By following these steps, your interviews can be effective in determining a person's compatibility with your organization. But interviews are typically unreliable in gauging trustworthiness in job applicants. Dishonest applicants often are quite adept at manipulating impressions.

Also be aware that interviews are time-consuming and expensive for screening large numbers of applicants. It's best to reserve the interview for the latter stages of the screening process, after you have eliminated less qualified candidates through other, more economical means. Even then, remember: If your screening process relies too heavily on interviews, it may produce discriminatory results.

Reference Checks

Most organizations investigate the applicant's background to determine if the application form or resumé is accurate or for a history of antisocial or counterproductive behavior.

Unfortunately traditional reference checking is becoming more difficult because increasing numbers of former employers volunteer as little information as possible in an effort to avoid lawsuits based on character defamation.

Worse, some employers may want to rid themselves of a thief quickly, and will not risk slowing his departure by informing other employers. Even when relatively minor crimes have been concerned, some firms believe that the guilty employee deserves a chance to move on and start over.

Finally, many employers fail to report crimes or to prosecute dishonest employees when they apprehend them, so the chances of obtaining accurate information on prior behavior are further diminished.

(This employee-privacy tradition, developed over the past fifteen years, is largely voluntary. Explicit legal restrictions on sharing employee information are in fact few. Corporate policies on privacy were developed mostly to head off suits by former employees.)

In addition to the current difficulties in obtaining candid information, reference checks often are done quickly, and by inexperienced people. In the hands of a thorough investigator, however, reference checks are among the most reliable methods to uncover valuable detail on an applicant's history.

The reference checker should talk to the applicant's actual former supervisors to determine the applicant's work habits, drive, motivation and skills, employment dates, and exact responsibilities, as well as his reasons for leaving. If possible, confirm earnings and salary growth. Ask about job-related health and attendance, any personal problems that interfered with the job, how the person accepted supervision, and how he got along with fellow workers. And ask if the former employer would rehire the applicant.

Prepare a checklist of these and other specific questions in advance from which to conduct the reference interview. You'll find a sample reference checklist on page 153.

Another approach to obtaining prior employment information is to have the applicant sign a waiver releasing the former employer from "any and all claims of liability arising out of the release of such information." Then mail the signed waiver and questionnaire with a self-addressed, stamped envelope to the former employer for completion. You'll find a sample reference waiver and questionnaire on page 154.

You also can use this approach to obtain information regarding an applicant's educational background. A school reference form is given on page 155.

Some employers use outside agencies to check references. Such checks usually include a review of the applicant's credit and criminal record, and, depending on your budget, also may include personal contact with former employers, neighbors, family, and friends. These services cost from $35 to $400 per investigation.

Criminal Record Checks

Most states (and several large city or county jurisdictions) have computerized repositories that contain arrest and conviction data as recorded by law enforcement and court agencies. These data bases vary considerably in comprehensiveness, historical depth, and geographical area covered.

Most human rights laws at state and federal levels prohibit use of arrest information, since it might discriminate against protected groups. Many states also prohibit consideration of felony convictions. And New York State substantially restricts the use of *any* conviction information for employment decisions.

Most employers find criminal record checks only rarely useful because so few applicants have actually been convicted of a crime and because many of the behavior problems that concern companies are not captured in criminal records. For instance, most drug users do not have criminal records (although more than half of all criminals use drugs).

Even in occupations that attract many job applicants with criminal backgrounds, difficulties with the quality and relevance of the records often are compounded by the delays encountered in obtaining them. Another obstacle to using criminal records is the varied and constantly changing laws across the fifty state jurisdictions regarding their access and use. The problem is particularly onerous, of course, for multistate employers who want to have uniform hiring standards across all their locations.

Despite these drawbacks, employers are feeling increased pressure to investigate criminal records as a precaution. Many corporate attorneys believe that company liability is less in the instance of an employee crime if criminal records have been reviewed before hire.

Although background data on an applicant's criminal past may raise issues about his trustworthiness and productivity, you must be careful about what role this information plays in your hiring decision. Relying on these reports without consideration of other, clearly job-related factors may produce discriminatory results. You must judge what these indicators of past behavior have to do with the applicant's qualifications for the job at hand, and be prepared to argue your conclusions in the event of a rejected applicant's challenge.

Biochemical Drug Testing

With substance abuse a widespread and serious problem in the American workplace, companies worry about its effects on productivity, company image, job safety, and employee theft. Employers with positions that require work around heavy machinery or precision of thought or movement are particularly sensitive to drug use on the job.

As described earlier, the growing number of drug-related lawsuits adds further urgency to the task of identifying substance abusers and keeping them out of certain jobs.

As proof of the scope of the problem, between 12 and 20 percent of today's job applicants don't pass biochemical drug screening tests.

Screening for drug use, however, raises a number of complex legal issues, like individual rights to privacy and company liability for drugged employee actions. The legal picture is confusing, with drug addicts, once hired, seemingly more protected in their right to keep their jobs and enjoy employee benefits than the occasional recreational user.

Drug testing also is expensive, ranging in price from $40 to $100 per person, and results may not be available for days.

Despite these disadvantages, growing numbers of companies feel compelled by concerns over liability and productivity to use biochemical drug tests for applicant screening after a conditional offer of employment has been made.

Polygraph Testing

Polygraph (or lie detector) testing attempts to identify whether or not an applicant is telling the truth about involvement in prior dishonest or illegal acts. The test involves questioning people while their physiological reactions—rates of respiration, blood pressure changes, and perspiration—are monitored with electrical equipment.

An examiner analyzing these changes attempts to estimate the likelihood that the applicant is telling the truth. Although the accuracy of this analysis is a matter of debate, the polygraph is quite effective in eliciting admissions of dishonest behavior: Most people who undergo such an examination believe that the instrument actually works—that it will register if they are lying.

Although the polygraph can be used to test employees allegedly involved in counterproductive acts, recent federal legislation prohibits most private employers from using the polygraph to screen job applicants. Employers exempt from this restriction—government agencies and employers that provide security services or that are involved in the manufacture or distribution of controlled substances—may elect to use the polygraph as a pre-employment screening tool, but they face the following disadvantages:

- Many applicants (and employees) consider the lie detector an invasion of privacy and a stressful experience, so its use may damage morale.
- Polygraph results may vary from examiner to examiner.
- Polygraphs are expensive. A well-trained and licensed examiner costs $100 an hour.
- Polygraphs are time-consuming, and often must be administered off premises.
- Polygraphs are not designed to *predict* counterproductive behavior, only to identify whether a person has been involved in crimes or substance abuse in the past. Therefore, a key question faces employers using the results of a polygraph test to make a hiring decision: What is the relation between the applicant's prior acts and future behavior? For instance, how long should an admission of purse-snatching while a youth be held against a person, and what is the relevance of this incident to the requirements of the job at hand?

Written Psychological Tests

Written psychological tests, or pencil-and-paper tests, inquire into the applicant's attitudes toward personal behavior and the work environment. Through statistical analysis based on thousands of responses, this technique predicts future behavior based on the applicant's attitudes and admissions of prior conduct. Pencil-and-paper integrity tests utilize the fact that dishonest, and honest, productive people don't think alike. For instance, people who are prone to dishonest behavior believe that dishonesty is commonplace, normal behavior, and that dishonest acts should not be disciplined.

The *Reid Report* is the original and most comprehensive instrument relying on attitudes to evaluate applicants for integrity, drug and alcohol abuse, and productivity. Its result is a probability indicating the likelihood that the applicant will engage in counterproductive acts on the job. It boasts high predictive accuracy in widely published and accepted psychological research. Users often see reductions in the rate of dishonest incidence on the job of 50 percent, with matching declines in employee drug use, turnover, and worker's compensation claims.

Such written tests are one of the least expensive methods of screening employees, costing between $10 and $20 per person. The Report is fast and convenient to administer, with results available instantly. It also offers a computerized record-keeping system to produce documentation of nondiscriminatory impact and thorough hiring procedures.

The quality of psychological tests can vary substantially from publisher to publisher. To select an effective and legally sound written psychological test, you need to know what to look for.

There are three characteristics that demonstrate whether a psychological test meets professional standards and conforms to the requirements of equal employment opportunity federal and state laws and regulations:

1. *Reliability.* The test measures consistently whatever it is designed to measure.

2. *Validity.* The test accurately predicts future behavior.

3. *Freedom from adverse impact.* The test passes protected groups (groups traditionally discriminated against because of age, sex, race, color, national origin, or religion) at a rate that is at least 80 percent of that for unprotected groups (usually whites or males).

Even if a test does create adverse impact based on the "80 percent" rule, it may still be legal to use if it is valid or job-related.

The failure of a job selection test to prove that it is valid and job-related, and that it does not discriminate against protected groups, can result in legal liability for both the test user and the test publisher.

For these reasons it is important that users of job selection tests purchase a product that has lengthy and well-accepted research.

Other considerations in selecting a test are as follows:

- *History.* The test publisher should be able to point to a long, unbroken series of favorable legal decisions in discrimination complaints, based on statistical proof.

- *Support.* The publisher should be willing and able to supply at no charge experienced guidance and well-recognized psychological and legal expert witnesses in the event of a complaint.

- *Knowledge of state laws.* The publisher should demonstrate strong knowledge of variations in state law as they are interpreted and put into practice.

- *Palatability.* The publisher should be able to demonstrate statistically that the test is not considered offensive by job applicants.
- *High Pass Rate.* If a test is inefficient, or attempts to track too many personality factors, it will reject a large portion of the applicant flow (as much as 70 percent) to identify a small number of low-risk applicants. In tight labor markets this poor pass rate will greatly increase recruiting costs.

Many pencil-and-paper psychological tests have recently appeared to capitalize on growing employee dishonesty and counterproductivity. To confirm a test's professional acceptance, you should consult independent review such as those found in Burros' *Eight Mental Measurement's Yearbook*, *The Encyclopedia of Psychology*, and *Keyser & Sweetland's Test Critiques*.

Quality psychological tests are increasingly found in effective screening programs, even those conducted by small businesses. But no single technique is perfect. Even highly accurate psychological tests will not guarantee that all applicants who pass will perform without incident on the job. Tests should be supplemented by reference checks and personal interviews.

CHOOSING THE RIGHT SCREENING TECHNIQUES FOR YOUR BUSINESS

Hiring trustworthy, productive employees is not difficult. The key is to choose the right screening techniques for your particular workplace and carry them out properly, in the optimal sequence.

The first step is to analyze carefully the skills and disposition needed for the job at hand and then decide the following: How important is the possibility of theft or substance abuse? To what degree will the job present the employee with opportunity to commit dishonest acts? Will the person be under close supervision, or lightly supervised? Answers to these questions will tell you how deeply you must delve into the applicant's past and attitudes.

Other factors to consider concern management of the screening process itself: How many jobs are you trying to fill at one time, or in a month, or in a year? How many applicants must you see to fill these jobs? How many man-hours can you dedicate to screening? Do you have the skilled personnel to do it, or must you bring in outside experts? What is your screening budget?

No matter what your final screening decisions are, experts recommend that you use at least several screening techniques to be sure you are obtaining sufficiently thorough, accurate information. Also important is the *sequence* of your screening steps: Start with the most economical

Table A.2
The Ideal Screening Sequence

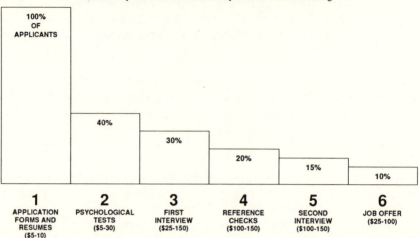

In the ideal screening sequence, the majority of applicants are eliminated in the
first few steps which are also the least expensive and time-consuming.

1	2	3	4	5	6
APPLICATION FORMS AND RESUMES ($5-10)	PSYCHOLOGICAL TESTS ($5-30)	FIRST INTERVIEW ($25-150)	REFERENCE CHECKS ($100-150)	SECOND INTERVIEW ($100-150)	JOB OFFER ($25-100)

technique and move through progressively costlier ones until you conclude with the most time-consuming, expensive screen. In this way you
will minimize your expenses by eliminating larger numbers of unsuitable
job applicants up front.

In calculating the cost of a screening technique, don't forget to estimate
the salary and overhead consumed in conducting applicant and reference
interviews. These expenses can be surprisingly high. A comprehensive
listing of the most commonly used screening techniques, with related
costs, advantages, and disadvantages appears in Table A.2. Refer to it
when constructing your screening program.

Finally, remember to standardize your procedure—use the same processes on all applicants, certainly on all those applying for the same job
function. Otherwise, you invite discrimination suits.

A popular combination of screening procedures includes the application form, a written psychological test, two interviews, and a reference
check organized in this economical sequence:

1. *Have applicants fill out well-designed, complete job application forms.*
2. *Review the forms.* Eliminate applicants who do not list the minimum
   education, skills, or experience required for the job. Also eliminate
   applicants who list a large number of jobs within a short period,
   or who list questionable reasons for leaving a previous job.
3. *Administer written psychological test.* Set up a quiet area for test
   administration. The test will take forty-five minutes to an hour to

complete, and there are several ways to obtain instant results— for instance by making a phone call or by scoring with a personal computer. Eliminate applicants who are not recommended.

4. *Conduct initial interviews.* By asking the right questions in this step, you can screen out unsuitable applicants and avoid time-consuming reference checks later. At the close of the interview tell the desirable applicant that you *will* be checking references.

5. *Check references.* Use this step to identify inconsistencies between interview and reference versions of the applicant's job history. Also probe for supervisors' opinions of the applicant's strengths and weaknesses.

6. *Conduct second interviews.* Change interviewers to get a fresh perspective and to avoid bias. Further investigate discrepancies and areas of concern raised during reference checking.

7. *Review results of screening measures.* After having eliminated the applicants who fell short on the application form, psychological test, and first interview results, compare the surviving applicants' ratings on their reference checks and final interview. (To rate candidates, set up a scoring system for the application form, interviews, and reference checks that assigns weights or numeric values to the key characteristics your job demands. Use the Post-Interview Evaluation Form on page 152 as a guide.) Then, make your hiring decision.

8. *Extend an offer of employment.* Now is the time to orient the new employee to the details of company policies on integrity, benefits, and work schedules.

WHAT DO I SAY TO REJECTED APPLICANTS?

How you handle rejected applicants can affect your company's future: If treated carelessly or with a lack of respect, they may dissuade other people from applying for a job with you, or from buying your products. Worse, they may file legal complaints. Although these people may not meet your requirements now, they might later. In short, you should treat them with dignity and leave them with a good feeling about your professionalism.

Always directly and promptly inform the rejected applicant as soon as you reach a decision to hire another, *and* your successful applicant has accepted your offer.

Whether you contact rejected candidates by phone or letter, try to emphasize their good points as you firmly explain your decision. *Never* tell them that they have the job or a good chance for it, only to reject them later.

A final word to the wise: Avoid identifying exactly which screening step they failed. Simply tell them you have found another applicant who "better fits the requirements of the job." Avoid hiring workers before you've investigated them. It's much more difficult, expensive, and potentially litigious to fire an employee than it is to decline an applicant.

HOW TO KEEP QUALITY EMPLOYEES

Congratulations. By following the steps outlined earlier, you are now hiring the highest-quality employees available. But how do you keep these valuable workers on board and productive? The first step toward solving this problem is to understand the reasons why *any* employee can become dissatisfied, disgruntled, unproductive, and dishonest.

Why Good Employees Go Wrong

The following factors highlight an important insight: Even employees with positive attitudes and no prior history of counterproductive behavior can go wrong under a certain combination of personal and workplace conditions.

Personal Situations. Conventional thought argues that financial needs arising from a variety of personal problems, like poor budget planning, drug use, gambling, alimony payments, or illness in the family, can force some employees into a series of dishonest acts. Perhaps surprisingly, recent psychological research tends to downplay the importance of situational pressures as an explanation for most deliberately counterproductive acts. There is little doubt, however, that personal crises like divorce or the death of a relative can seriously impair performance.

Frustrated Ambition. Employees who think that they have been made false promises of advancement, or who think that the company is indifferent to their efforts or needs find it easier to rationalize acts of dishonesty or laxness on the job. After all, the company hasn't kept its end of the bargain, so why should they?

Low-Risk Opportunity. When an act of theft requires little effort, or when the chances of being caught or prosecuted appear remote, employees are more likely to become dishonest. Certain positions that require working directly with merchandise or cash with minimal supervision obviously increase opportunities for dishonesty.

Attitude. Attitudes, formed at an early age, are accurate predictors of performance on the job. Some people are simply more honest and committed to the work ethic than others. Rigorous applicant-screening processes are designed to identify those who are less honest before they are hired.

Identifying and Defeating Counterproductive Conditions

At the root of much employee demoralization is inattentive or indifferent management. Managers can frustrate productive employees by smothering their projects with delays and red tape and by ignoring their personal circumstances or their need to grow into greater responsibility.

Managers also can fail to recognize and reward hard work, causing employees to "get even" by engaging in counterproductive acts.

Inattentive managers don't recognize the adverse effects even a few bad employees have on good ones. An extreme example of this is the company that is forced to close down after a major internal theft, throwing many productive employees out of work. Such an occurrence is not so rare; one-third of all business failures are caused by such employee dishonesty.

Other ways bad workers can affect good ones are subtler. For instance, the job can become unpleasant for productive employees who dislike working alongside someone they know or suspect is deliberately counterproductive. They get distracted, too, when they see someone avoiding work or stealing while others are playing by the rules.

In fact, productive employees often feel caught in the middle when forced into this situation, and will choose to resign rather than face an unpleasant choice between informing on a counterproductive co-worker who may even be a friend and joining in a conspiracy of dishonesty.

Managers also frequently underestimate how quickly employees recognize when misconduct is tolerated or overlooked. The best workers will leave poorly managed companies precisely because their personal standards are high. Those who stay may yield to the temptation to commit counterproductive acts without fear of discipline.

The task, then, is to create a positive work environment by taking steps to encourage honesty and strong morale. You must establish firm expectations and standards of conduct, reinforcement for correct behavior, discipline for counterproductive behavior, and genuine concern by management for the welfare of employees.

Creating a Positive Work Environment

1. *Select honest employees.* Start by emphasizing the importance of integrity in each step of the selection process. The very elements of an effective pre-employment screening system send a clear message to the new employee that hiring honest, dependable, hardworking employees is a top priority.

2. *Make a team of your employees.* Good managers create a sense of teamwork and concern for joint goals among their subordinates. They encourage employees to take personal pride in their contributions and

the organization's effectiveness through a variety of techniques: special awards and incentives for outstanding effort or performance, group outings, and company or department events that encourage employees to relax and become familiar with the personal side of their managers and co-workers. This recognition encourages employees to return the favor by working hard. Such employees also are less likely to leave the "family" in search of "greener pastures."

A related issue is compensation. All personnel should feel that their pay is fair relative to what others receive for similar work, and is tied to job responsibilities, performance levels, and seniority. Perceptions of inequitable pay are a major source of disgruntlement. When legitimate pay differences exist, managers should carefully explain the reasons behind them so that the employee can place the disparity in perspective.

3. *Develop a manager's code of ethics.* Open discussion among managers to establish a code of ethics raises awareness of honest, fair business practices. These discussions allow company executives to identify circumstances that could lead to compromised behavior, and to develop a consensus on appropriate punishment. Because this *process* is more important than the written code itself, it is wise to repeat it every two years or so. That way you can better assure that your managers will fulfill their responsibility to act as ethical role models for all employees.

While it's important that managers know acceptable rules of conduct, avoid overly elaborate, legalistic language in your code. It could send the message that you don't trust your employees, or that the company's ethical commitment is an empty formality. The key is a set of clear positions developed through participative management. Another advantage to this approach is that managers who have a voice in corporate decisions are better able and more motivated to carry them out.

4. *Involve your rank and file in establishing written anti-theft and drug abuse policies.* New employees should immediately be exposed to this written statement. It describes prohibited behavior and the disciplinary steps that will follow. It is widely displayed and frequently referenced in company communications. One such policy reads, in part: "Whenever an incident of drug abuse or dishonesty occurs, we will identify which company rules have been violated and who has violated them. Listed below are company rules of conduct, and the disciplinary actions that will result if they are violated." Some policies also outline steps to rehabilitate the drug or alcohol abuser before disciplinary actions are taken.

Periodic meetings that allow employees to discuss ways in which the policy may be improved are further opportunities to reinforce the message that counterproductive acts will not be tolerated. These sessions also are valuable for stressing the adverse effects that such acts have on fellow workers, as well as on the company.

By educating employees about these issues and inviting their help in solving the problem, you encourage them to take responsibility for the success of the program. Some companies go further: They describe the problem, demonstrate that it exists, and then ask the employees to pinpoint its causes and develop solutions.

Training films and exercises available today plant important antitheft seeds. Many businesses use videos on internal theft topics that alert employees to circumstances that invite theft, suspicious behavior, ways to deal with others' counterproductive actions, and the consequences of these incidents for all parties.

5. *Use surveys to detect counterproductivity.* Employees are more likely to engage in dishonest acts when they see others bending the rules or breaking them. A supervisor who steals or sloughs off encourages subordinates to think that they have the right to do the same. Worse, this supervisor cannot now easily discipline a subordinate who commits the same act, in effect mimicking the boss. This caution applies to the unauthorized use of company services or assets and time theft, as well as tangible theft.

To determine if such activity is occurring, many companies survey individual employees confidentially, thereby assessing levels of disgruntlement and knowledge or admissions of dishonest acts. Surveys also can enlist employee suggestions in ways to discourage such behavior. An example of a powerful and convenient pencil-and-paper employee survey is the *Reid Survey*, the first such instrument commonly used by industry.

6. *Create timely and accurate internal controls.* Good controls make counterproductive behavior less convenient and more likely to be detected. Effective controls also quickly report deviations from the norm, before further damage is perpetrated and before valuable evidence is obscured. Controls can take the form of procedural, policy, or physical systems.

Examples of procedural controls are inventory systems, shipping and receiving procedures, and the standard methods by which damaged or returned goods are processed and stored. Tight procedural controls signal to the employee that the company values its assets and the employee should too.

An example of a policy control is an absenteeism program. A certain level of absenteeism is an organizational fact of life. But this level can be kept low by a simple and carefully monitored attendance recording system. Rewards for perfect attendance are a common feature of successful absenteeism programs.

Physical controls include physical inventories, cash counts, investigative shoppers, electronic surveillance systems, garment tags, two-way mirrors, alarms, an efficient workplace floor plan, secure trash disposal, good lighting, and neat housekeeping. All these controls serve two purposes: to catch or foil the counterproductive employee and, perhaps more important, to signal management's resolution to protect the company.

The characteristics of good inventory and cash controls are speed and sensitivity. They act as "trip wires," setting off a flare for further investigation. Standard bookkeeping or accounting systems seldom can react before serious damage occurs; they just document the damage. Instead, develop simple systems, like a visual check mark on an inventory bin, that bypass accounting procedures.

7. *Develop a grievance system that provides "due process."* In addition to well-defined disciplinary procedures, every organization should have a grievance procedure to protect employees from unfair supervisory actions. By treating employees fairly, it is consistent to expect them to follow high standards of integrity.

8. *Reward employees for reducing theft.* Financial incentives like bounties are effective. So are profit-sharing arrangements based on reduced rates of shrinkage. When other employees are observant, it is difficult to commit the secret act of theft.

Recent surveys confirm that more than 50 percent of larger companies pay employees for reduced shrinkage. Entry-level employees respond best to cash; middle and upper management may prefer recognition. Most participants in bounty programs want to remain anonymous. Some employees, although uninterested in personally accepting a reward, are willing to have it donated to a favorite charity or employee fund.

9. *Frequently evaluate and reward employee performance.* This is a central element in the employer–employee contract and the key to strong morale. An atmosphere of mutual respect makes it difficult to rationalize dishonest acts. Conduct structured performance reviews as often as quarterly, and be prepared to acknowledge superior accomplishment just as frequently with tangible benefits.

Keeping quality employees means creating a healthy work environment in which employee behavior is rapidly and appropriately rewarded or disciplined as the situation demands. The research findings are clear: Your company's investment in the steps necessary to achieve this environment will be returned many-fold by a productive, honest work force.

Table A.3
Summary of Job Applicant Techniques

SUMMARY OF JOB APPLICANT SCREENING TECHNIQUES

PROCEDURE	COST PER USE	STRENGTHS	WEAKNESSES
Personal Interview	$25-$150	Measures verbal skill, neatness, compatibility, apparent knowledge and motivation.	Unreliable on integrity. Expensive. Can be discriminatory.
Motor Vehicle Record (MVR)	$2-$5	Cheap. Valuable if convictions recorded.	Valid only if job requires driving. Can be slow: up to three weeks.
Credit Check	$5-$15	Cheap, fast.	You must demonstrate relationship between job and credit history. Discriminatory?
State and County Criminal Records	$0-$50	Valuable if job-related convictions recorded.	Convictions are rare. Often slow. Some states will not release data. Beware of inaccuracies.
Reference Check	$50-$150	Verifies history of prior achievements.	Many companies have "no talk" policies. Takes skilled investigator.
Psychological Test	$5-$30	Cheap, non-discriminatory, fast, strong documentation.	Accuracy depends on vendor. Some tests fail too many candidates.
Polygraph Interrogation	$40-$100	Unsurpassed on specific incident investigations.	Federal law prohibits use for most employers. Invasive, time-consuming, expensive.
Psychological Stress Evaluation, Graphology	$25-$50	Some users swear by them.	Not considered reliable or valid.
Background Check	$100+	Thorough history of prior behavior.	What aspects of background are job-related, especially for young applicants? Slow. Expensive.
Drug Test	$15-$100	Accurate on recent drug use.	Invasive, court challenges. Expensive. Is off-the-job drug use relevant?
Store Mutual Protective Association	$1-$2	Database on criminal employees reported by retailer members. Cheap per use, fast.	Covers only individuals reported by retailers. Large member fee ($1000+).

Table A.4
Post-Interview Evaluation Form

Confidential

POST-INTERVIEW EVALUATION FORM

Applicant Name _____ Position _____ Date ____/____/____

Employment Location _____

Characteristics

1. **Ability to do the job**

   Low | 1 | 2 | 3 | 4 | 5 | 6 | 7 | 8 | 9 | 10 | High

2. **Motivation**

   Low | 1 | 2 | 3 | 4 | 5 | 6 | 7 | 8 | 9 | 10 | High

3. **Willingness to assume responsibility**

   Low | 1 | 2 | 3 | 4 | 5 | 6 | 7 | 8 | 9 | 10 | High

4. **Personality that fits the job**

   Poor | 1 | 2 | 3 | 4 | 5 | 6 | 7 | 8 | 9 | 10 | Perfect

5. **Initiative/Creativity**

   Low | 1 | 2 | 3 | 4 | 5 | 6 | 7 | 8 | 9 | 10 | High

6. **Loyalty**

   Low | 1 | 2 | 3 | 4 | 5 | 6 | 7 | 8 | 9 | 10 | High

7. **Perseverance**

   Low | 1 | 2 | 3 | 4 | 5 | 6 | 7 | 8 | 9 | 10 | High

8. **Cooperation**

   Low | 1 | 2 | 3 | 4 | 5 | 6 | 7 | 8 | 9 | 10 | High

9. **Self-reliance**

   Low | 1 | 2 | 3 | 4 | 5 | 6 | 7 | 8 | 9 | 10 | High

10. **Emotional maturity**

    Poor | 1 | 2 | 3 | 4 | 5 | 6 | 7 | 8 | 9 | 10 | Good

11. **Self expression**

    Poor | 1 | 2 | 3 | 4 | 5 | 6 | 7 | 8 | 9 | 10 | Excellent

12. **Moral standards**

    Low | 1 | 2 | 3 | 4 | 5 | 6 | 7 | 8 | 9 | 10 | High

Overall Impressions/Comments: _____

_____

TOTAL RATING: (add items 1-12) ☐

AVERAGE RATING: (divide total by 12) ☐   INTERVIEWER: _____

Table A.5
Applicant Reference Check List

Confidential

APPLICANT REFERENCE CHECK LIST
(Phone Interview Version)

Applicant Name _____

Company _____ Telephone No. _____

Name of Person Contacted _____ Contact's Position _____

1. Was _____ employed by your company? Yes ( ) No ( )
    (Name of applicant)

2. Dates of Employment. From: _____/_____/_____ To: _____/_____/_____

3. What job did applicant have when he/she started work for you? _____

4. What was applicant's job when he/she left? _____

5. What were applicant's strong points? _____

6. What were applicant's weak points? _____

7. How did applicant accept supervision? _____

8. How would you rate applicant's honesty? _____

9. Has applicant sustained any physical disabilities that would impair performance on this job? Yes ( ) No ( )

10. Was applicant ever convicted of a crime while in your employ? Yes ( ) No ( )

11. How well did applicant get along with fellow workers? _____

12. How well did applicant get along with customers? _____

13. How much time did applicant lose from work? _____

14. Was applicant — Laid Off? ( ) Discharged? ( ) Resigned? ( )

15. Explain the reason for applicant leaving your employ. _____

16. Would you rehire applicant? Yes ( ) No ( )

17. Where was applicant previously employed? _____

FOR TRUCK OR AUTO DRIVER APPLICANTS:

18. Did applicant drive: Locally ( )   Out-Of-Town ( )
                          Truck ( )   Semi-Trailer ( )   Auto ( )

19. What was applicant's traffic accident history? _____

20. What was applicant's traffic violations history? _____

21. Was applicant's license ever suspended? Yes ( ) No ( )

    Reason for suspension _____

22. Other Remarks _____

Reference Checker's Name _____ Date _____/_____/_____

Table A.6
Employment Reference waiver and questionnaire

Confidential

EMPLOYMENT REFERENCE WAIVER AND QUESTIONNAIRE
FROM: (Company name and address)

TO: _____   Re: _____ (Applicant Name) _____

_____   Maiden Name _____

_____   S.S. # _____

_____   Job Title _____

Employed From ___/___/___ To ___/___/___

Dear Sir or Madam:

    I have applied for a position of responsibility with the above-named company. I hereby authorize you to provide this company with any and all information contained in my personnel file or known to you about me. I hereby release you from any and all claims of liability arising out of the release of such information.

Signature _____ ___/___/___
                                                             Date

------------------ FORMER EMPLOYER: TEAR HERE AND RETAIN TOP HALF ------------------
PLEASE RETURN BOTTOM HALF TO ABOVE COMPANY

Firm Name _____

Former Employee _____

S.S. # _____

Employed As _____

Starting   Leaving

Date ___/___/___   Date ___/___/___

Reason for Leaving?   Discharged ( )
                         Laid Off   ( )
                         Quit   ( )

Eligible for Rehire?   Yes   ( )
                         No   ( )

	Excel.	Good	Fair	Poor
Quality of Work				
Quantity of Work				
Ability to Do Other Work				
Attendance				
General Conduct				
Cooperation				
Personal Habits				
Honesty				

FURTHER REMARKS ON ABOVE: _____

_____

_____

GENERAL COMMENTS: Please feel free to write below any information which will assist in placing this applicant in a position which would be of greatest benefit to him or her, and to us:

_____

_____

_____

_____

_____   _____ _____ ___/___/___

Please Print Your Name Here   Signature   Title   Date

Table A.7
School Reference Form

Confidential

SCHOOL REFERENCE FORM
FROM: (Company name and address)

TO: RECORD OFFICE

_____ School   Re: _____ (Applicant Name) _____

_____   Maiden Name _____

_____   Class of _____

Dear Sir or Madam:

    I have applied for a position of responsibility with the above-named company. I hereby authorize you to supply this company with any and all information contained in my record file or known to you about me. I hereby release you from any and all claims of liability arising out of the dissemination of such information.

Signature _____   ____/____/____
                                                        Date

- SCHOOL: TEAR HERE AND RETAIN TOP HALF -
PLEASE RETURN BOTTOM HALF TO ABOVE COMPANY

Student Name _____

School Name _____   Date of Last Attendance _____/_____/_____

Circle Highest Grade Completed:

    6   7   8   9   10   11   12   College   1   2   3   4

Did Student Graduate? _____   (If Not, Why?) _____

Grade Point or Scholastic Average _____   Class Rank _____ No. in Class _____

Please Rate: Attendance Record _____   Punctuality Record_____

                Maturity _____   Individual Effort _____

                Ability to work with others _____

Any Suspensions? _____   (If Yes, Why?) _____

Was Student Ever Expelled? _____   (If Yes, Why?) _____

Other Disciplinary Problems? _____   (If Yes, Please Explain) _____

GENERAL COMMENTS: Please feel free to give us any further information which will help us in placing this individual in the position which would be of greatest benefit to him or her, and to us. Information on extra-curricular activities, special honors, or class offices held is helpful.

_____

_____

_____

_____

_____   _____ _____   ____/____/____
Please Print Your Name Here   Signature   Title   Date

Employee Theft

Employee theft is all too common at the workplace. Although it is difficult to accept, many trusted employees will steal cash, goods, tools, equipment, supplies, time, services, information, or anything else of value from the business if given the opportunity. It has been estimated that as much as 80 percent of all crime-related losses suffered by businesses are due to employee theft. The following suggestions are intended to reduce the opportunity for the crime.

PREVENTION

- Keep accurate records on the movement of cash and goods from the time they enter the business until they leave.
- Keep an accurate inventory system and have it checked regularly by someone other than the person responsible for maintaining it.
- Periodically monitor cash register transactions to assure that they are being handled correctly.
- Devise a tracking system to measure business volume by day of week and time of day. Check the pattern on a regular basis to determine if income is dropping by these and other variables.
- Do not allow employees to handle their own sales transactions.
- Have a clear-cut policy on employee discounts and fringe benefits.

This material is taken from *Crime Prevention for Virginia Businesses*. It was written by Virginia's Crime Prevention Manual Task Force.

- Limit access to valuables to appropriate employees. Strict key control should be used for access to business premises, storerooms, and display areas. Other employees who need access to sensitive areas on an irregular basis should be required to sign for keys.
- Employees' personal belongings, such as coats, purses, and packages, should be stored in a safe place with limited access, away from merchandise easily concealed.
- Establish a policy of checking employees and their belongings as they leave work. Such checks can be done daily or on an irregular, but unannounced basis.
- Search trash on a regular basis to prevent goods from being carried out with it. Flatten boxes to eliminate possible hiding places for merchandise.
- Employee parking should be located away from the building to deny easy access during the workday for the purpose of concealing property.
- Limit and monitor the number of exits so that employees will find it difficult to carry merchandise out of the building without your knowledge.
- Put locked screens on the windows to deny the opportunity to pass merchandise through them.
- If possible, make shipping and receiving two separate operations. If impractical, assure that the operation is monitored by someone in the business who can detect irregularities.
- Establish a policy that rewards employees who uncover security problems.
- If practical, have different employees handle purchasing and billing/accounts payable. Monitor these activities to determine if accepted accounting principles are being applied.

DEVELOPING POLICIES

It is necessary to prepare a policy statement that informs employees that theft of company-owned property will not be tolerated and that violators will be dealt with severely, resulting in dismissal and/or prosecution. The policy statement should be written in a straightforward, concise manner; furnished to each employee and explained; signed by each employee as a condition of employment; and enforced uniformly.

HIRING PRACTICES

The most important step that can be taken to prevent employee theft is to hire honest people who have not previously been dismissed from other companies for theft. Regardless of the position being filled, have the candidate complete an application form. Check all information for accuracy. Check all references including personal, work, and credit. Call the last and next to last employer and ask the following questions about the worker:

- When did the employee begin working for you?
- When did the employee leave your company?
- Was the worker terminated, asked to resign, or leave voluntarily?
- If he or she did not resign voluntarily, what were the circumstances surrounding the separation?
- What were the employee's habits with respect to attendance, promptness, relation with other employees and supervisors, and job performance?
- Were the wages of the employee ever garnished?
- Did the employee have a history of drug or alcohol abuse?
- Was the employee ever accused of theft from your business or of assault of a customer or client?

If you cannot verify all pertinent information or you discover dishonesty, do not hire the person.

EMPLOYEE ORIENTATION

As employees are hired, help them to understand that they are integral parts of the business and that by working hard to make the business successful, they will receive a fair wage, job security, respect, consideration, and gratitude. Explain that you are not questioning their integrity, but rather helping them to understand the importance of good security habits so they will be valuable employees.

By discussing security with new employees you will help them to recognize management's interest in it and perceive that controls have been instituted to detect dishonest employees. They will, therefore, be more likely to comply with security guidelines established by management and less likely to engage in theft.

PROFILING THE EMPLOYEE THIEF

One of the responsibilities of supervisors is to know subordinates well enough to recognize personal problems that may have a negative effect on the business. Awareness of problems and personality traits can enable management to assist the employee through a personal crisis as well as to target employees for closer scrutiny. Some employee activities or personality traits that should warrant attention are the following:

- Evidence of a personal crisis, such as illness, divorce, or other problems in the family
- Alcohol or drug abuse
- Obsessive gambling
- Financial difficulties
- Disgruntled,"overworked and underpaid"
- Dishonest tendencies in job activities
- Poor attitude toward security
- Quick to accuse fellow workers of dishonesty
- Living beyond the means of job income
- Close relations with other employees, such as dating, strong relationship, and family
- Frequently visited by friends and family at work
- Personal and overly friendly relations with suppliers and customers
- Working long hours and assuming and guarding responsibilities
- Volunteering to open and lock up each day or requesting hours and duties that are most susceptible to criminal opportunity

EMPLOYEE THEFT PROCEDURES

If you suspect an employee or a group of employees of stealing, it is suggested that you proceed with caution and collect as much evidence as possible. The following steps are recommended:

- Carefully choose the key employees with whom you confide concerning thefts by other employees.
- Establish a control situation so you can positively identify the property stolen as belonging to your business.
- Keep written documentation concerning the theft of property by an employee, including the date and time, property missing, who had access to it, and other circumstances.
- If the problem is pervasive, hire an undercover operative to work in your business to identify the people involved.
- Once you have established that property or assets are being stolen, report your findings to your law enforcement agency.

PROSECUTION

When you uncover a thief, the correct course of action is to notify your law enforcement agency and be prepared to prosecute. Simple dismissal is sending the wrong message to other employees. Prosecution becomes a strong deterrent to others. All too often employees are fired from one job and quickly hired by someone else because there is nothing in their background to indicate that they were fired for stealing.

What Motivates Employees? Workers and Supervisors Give Different Answers

Kenneth A. Kovach

Which do workers value more: interesting work or good wages? Supervisors think they know the answer, but forty years of survey results prove that they don't.

Why do workers work? Industrial psychologists and management experts have sought the answer to this question for many years. If a company knows why its employees come to work on time, stay with the company for their full working lives, and are productive, then it might be able to ensure that all of its employees behave in that way. Such a company would have a decided marketplace advantage over competitors suffering from absenteeism, costly retraining programs, and production slowdowns.

WHICH DO WORKERS WANT: INTERESTING WORK OR GOOD WAGES?

How can we discover why workers work? One obvious way is to ask employees what they prefer in their work environment. When we asked 1,000 industrial employees this question, we found that the item most frequently cited was "interesting work."

If this is the answer, then all that is necessary is to make all of the work in industry interesting. Then we will have happy, productive employees who come to work on time and don't quit. Unfortunately not

Reprinted from *Business Horizons*, September-October 1987. Copyright 1987 by the Foundation for the School of Business at Indiana University. Used with permission.

all jobs can be made interesting. More important, what is interesting to one person may not be interesting to someone else.

If direct supervisors are able to recognize the differences between their employees, then perhaps they can make sure that everyone is in a job that he or she finds interesting. However, when supervisors were asked what they thought their employees wanted from their jobs, the supervisors claimed that their workers' highest preference was not for interesting work, but for good wages. If the immediate supervisors are to be believed, all a company has to do is to make sure that it pays good wages to all its employees.

Good wages are probably easier to offer than interesting work, but the employees say that salary alone doesn't rank extremely high on their list of preferences. Thus there are some differences in how managers view the reasons workers work and how workers view the reasons they work.

This article compares results of three surveys concerning employee and supervisory rankings of ten motivational items, discusses individual differences between groups of employees and supervisors, and looks at the manipulation of reward systems.

FORTY YEARS OF SURVEYS

In 1946 industrial employees were asked to rank ten "job reward" factors in terms of personal preference. The results were as follows:

1. Full appreciation of work done
2. Feeling of being in on things
3. Sympathetic help with personal problems
4. Job security
5. Good wages
6. Interesting work
7. Promotion and growth in the organization
8. Personal loyalty to employees
9. Good working conditions
10. Tactful discipline[1]

A similar questionnaire was given to industrial employees in 1981 and again in 1986.

By 1981 what workers wanted had changed. "Interesting work" was in first position and "sympathetic help with personal problems" had dropped to the ninth slot. By 1986 the list looked like this:

1. Interesting work
2. Full appreciation of work done
3. Feeling of being in on things
4. Job security
5. Good wages
6. Promotion and growth in organization
7. Good working conditions
8. Personal loyalty to employees
9. Tactful discipline
10. Sympathetic help with personal problems

The workers surveyed in 1946 came from a different environment than today's factory workers. America had come out of a depression and had just gone through a war. In 1986, after almost forty years of relative prosperity and a rise in the standard of living beyond the imagination of workers in 1946, it is not surprising that what workers want from their work had changed.

MOTIVATION, MASLOW, AND HERZBERG

The late psychologist A. H. Maslow organized human needs on five general levels.[2] In ascending order these are as follows:

- Physiological needs (food, water, sex, shelter)
- Safety needs (protection)
- Social needs (belonging, acceptance)
- Ego needs (achievement, status, appreciation)
- Self-actualization needs (need to realize one's potential)

The first three needs can be considered basic, or "deficit," needs. When these basic needs are satisfied, then the ego and self-actualization needs are pursued.

Frederick Herzberg's two-factor theory, also known as the motivation-hygiene theory, divides need satisfactions into extrinsic and intrinsic factors.[3] The extrinsic factors—such as salary, working conditions, and job security—lead to job dissatisfaction if not met, but will not necessarily contribute to job satisfaction when they are met. The intrinsic factors—such as the work itself, achievement, and recognition—are the actual motivators; they fulfill a person's need for psychological growth. The extrinsic factors, on the other hand, merely prevent dissatisfaction.

If we relate the list of employee ratings to Maslow's hierarchy of needs or to Herzberg's hygiene theory, it becomes fairly obvious that organizations in the U.S. industrial sector have done a better job of satisfying the basic, or "deficit," needs of their workers than they have in satisfying the ego or self-fulfillment needs.[4]

In the 1946, 1981, and 1986 studies supervisors were asked to rank job rewards as they believed employees would rank them. Their rankings remained almost the same for each year. They are as follows:

1. Good wages
2. Job security
3. Promotion and growth in the organization
4. Good working conditions
5. Interesting work
6. Personal loyalty to employees
7. Tactful discipline
8. Full appreciation of work done
9. Sympathetic help with personal problems
10. Feeling of being in on things

The supervisor's rankings show that not only have they not changed over the past forty years their collective perception of factors that motivate employees, but also that they don't realize the importance of Maslow's hierarchy of needs or Herzberg's extrinsic and intrinsic factors in motivation. Most important, a comparison of the rankings shows that supervisors have an inaccurate perception of what motivates employees.

MANAGERS AND MOTIVATION

Assuming that they are aware of almost four decades of research, why have managers chosen to ignore the theories of motivation? Specifically, why do managers continually place wages at the top of their hierarchy and the other motivators, which both Maslow and Herzberg consider essential for job satisfaction, at the bottom? Several explanations are possible for supervisors' apparent neglect of the conclusions drawn from the research of behavioral scientists.

One reason could be that supervisors believe that employees find an interest in money and other basic needs socially undesirable and therefore pay lip service to more socially acceptable factors such as interesting work. On the other hand, it is possible that employees are better witnesses to their own feelings than are their supervisors.

Another reason for the disparity may be that managers choose rewards for which they are less responsible. For example, pay raises usually are determined by formalized organizational policies, not by the personal relations between supervisors and employees. Thus supervisors can "pass the buck" when it comes time to assign blame for poor levels of employee motivation. These explanations are largely untested. Another theory that may explain this phenomenon can be called "self-reference." Managers offer rewards or behave toward workers in ways that would motivate *them*, but these are not necessarily the rewards and behaviors that will motivate *their employees*.

David McClelland found that most supervisors are high achievers who are interested in concrete measures—money—that reflect how well they have done.[5] For managers, money is a quantifiable way of keeping score.

In 1946 there was a significant difference between the way supervisors ranked employee rewards and the rankings made by employees themselves; there also was a significant difference between the two in 1981 and 1986. Thus managers appear to remain out of tune with the desires of their employees. Despite a tremendous volume of behavioral research into what motivates employees, supervisory self-reference is as much of a problem today as it was after World War II—a sad commentary on the implementation of research results in the workplace.

HOW WORKERS' VALUES DIFFER

The 1986 survey divided employees into various categories, something the earlier surveys did not do. Just as there are differences between which employees want overtime, there also may be differences between categories of employees based on sex, age, income level, job type, and organization level. Table A.8 shows the subgroups studied in the 1986 survey, and Table A.9 analyzes subset data and makes it possible for the responses of each subset to be compared with those of the entire group of 1,000 employees. Note that supervisors are not included in the subgroups—only the 1,000 employees.

MALE/FEMALE

When the responses of men and women were analyzed, no significant statistical difference was found in the preferences of the two groups. Women, however, put "full appreciation of work" in first place, whereas men put it second. Female employees may place greater importance on interpersonal relations and communication than do male employees, a difference that should be noted by managers. Women in the workplace have different problems than do men; many are still trying to cope with their traditional roles as housewives along with their roles as workers.

Table A.8
Statistics for the 1986 Survey

1,000 Employees (Industrial Sector)	100 Supervisors* (First and Second Level)
Sex	**Sex**
M = 622	M = 76
F = 378	F = 24
Age	**Age**
Under 30 = 202	Under 30 = 16
31-40 = 348	31-40 = 29
41-50 = 325	41-50 = 40
Over 50 = 125	Over 50 = 15
Income Level	**Income Level**
Under $12,000 = 135	Under $16,000 = 6
$12,001-$18,000 = 360	$16,001-$22,000 = 34
$18,001-$25.000 = 334	$22.001=$30,000 = 39
Over $25,000 = 171	Over $30,000 = 21
Job Type	**Job Type Supervised**
Blue-collar unskilled = 350	Blue-collar unskilled = 31
Blue-collar skilled = 291	Blue-collar skilled = 27
White-collar unskilled = 206	White-collar unskilled = 23
White-collar skilled = 113	White-collar skilled = 19
Organization Level	**Organizational Level Supervised**
Lower Nonsupervisory = 418	Lower Nonsupervisory = 34
Middle Nonsupervisory = 359	Middle Nonsupervisory = 37
Higher Nonsupervisory = 139	Higher Nonsupervisory = 29

*Supervisors surveyed are directly connected with employees surveyed.

This possible role conflict could cause women to seek more appreciation of work.

Age Group

Four age groups were analyzed: under 30, 31–40, 41–50, and over 50. The under–30 group showed the greatest disparity in its distribution from the total responses of all groups but the greatest similarity to the supervisors' estimate of how employees would respond. The difference between how the under–30 group responded when compared with each of the other age groups is statistically significant.

The under–30 group chose good wages, job security, and promotion and growth as their first three choices. This could indicate that these new workers have not yet fulfilled their basic needs according to Maslow.

Table A.9
What Workers Want, Ranked by Subgroups (1986 Survey)

			Sex		Age				Income Level				Job Type				Org. Level		
	Supervisors	Employees	Men	Women	Under 30	31-40	41-50	Over 50	Under $12,000	$12,000-$18,000	$18,001-$25,000	Over $25,000	Blue-Collar Unskilled	Blue-Collar Skilled	White-Collar Unskilled	White-Collar Skilled	Lower Nonsupervisory	Middle Nonsupervisory	Higher Nonsupervisory
Interesting work	5	1	1	2	4	2	3	1	5	2	1	1	2	1	1	2	3	1	1
Full appreciation of work done	8	2	1	3	5	3	2	2	4	3	3	2	1	6	3	1	4	2	2
Feeling of being in on things	10	3	2	3	6	4	1	3	6	1	2	4	5	2	5	4	5	3	3
Job security	2	4	5	4	2	1	4	7	2	4	4	3	4	3	7	5	2	4	6
Good wages	1	5	4	5	1	5	5	8	1	5	6	8	3	4	6	6	1	6	8
Promotion and growth in org.	3	6	6	6	3	6	8	9	3	6	5	7	6	5	4	3	6	5	5
Good working conditions	4	7	7	7	7	7	7	4	8	7	7	6	9	7	2	7	7	7	4
Personal loyalty to employees	7	8	8	8	9	9	6	5	7	8	8	5	8	9	9	8	8	8	7
Tactful discipline	9	9	9	9	8	10	9	10	10	9	9	10	7	9	9	8	9	9	10
Sympathetic help with personal problems	6	10	10	10	10	8	10	6	9	10	10	9	10	8	8	10	10	10	9

When the under–30 group is compared with the other groups, it is interesting to note that the 31–40 group still place job security high on their hierarchy of values but that this basic need becomes less important as one moves up through the age groups. Thus industry seems to do well in taking care of the basic needs of employees, at least for those who stay past their fortieth birthday. If Maslow is to be believed, older workers should then place more emphasis on their social and ego needs, their lower order needs being fulfilled. This would explain why workers over 50 place "sympathetic help with personal problems," "good working conditions," and "personal loyalty to employees" moderately high on their lists of preferences—certainly higher than do younger employees.

Income

The low-income group (under $12,000) showed a response pattern that was quite different from the total employee responses but similar to supervisory expectations. The responses also were statistically different from the other income groups.

Like younger employees, the low-income group placed "good wages," "job security," and "promotion and growth in the organization" in the primary positions.

The next two income levels (through $25,000) strongly resembled each other. They differed from the low-income group in that they placed "good wages," "job security," and "promotion and growth in the organization" in the middle position in their list of preferences.

Interestingly, the over-$25,000 group put "job security" third in importance. Perhaps increased affluence also increases the desire to retain it.

Job Types

A comparison of the blue-collar unskilled responses and white-collar unskilled responses showed significant differences. The unskilled blue-collar group gave top ranking to "full appreciation of work done," "interesting work," and "good wages," whereas the unskilled white-collar worker showed a greater interest in "interesting work," "good working conditions," and "appreciation of work done." The unskilled blue-collar worker was slightly more interested in "job security" than the unskilled white-collar worker, whereas the unskilled white-collar worker placed more value on "promotion and growth in the organization."

Fewer differences emerge when comparing the skilled blue-collar with the skilled white-collar worker. The most significant difference is that skilled blue-collar workers do not seem to place as much value on "full appreciation of work done." It may be that skilled blue-collar workers are intrinsically content with their work because, in the majority of cases, their tasks are well defined and self-contained. The tasks of white-collar workers, on the other hand, tend to be more open-ended, and the worker is more dependent on supervisory feedback for the definition and assessment of the job.

"Job security" was of significant importance for the blue-collar skilled worker, who ranked it third, whereas "promotion and growth in the organization" was ranked third by the white-collar skilled.

The most significant difference between blue-collar unskilled and blue-collar skilled is the value they place on "full appreciation of work done." The skilled worker rated this factor sixth out of ten, whereas the unskilled worker placed it first in importance.

White-collar unskilled and white-collar skilled workers rated "good working conditions" significantly differently. The unskilled worker placed working conditions second in importance, whereas the skilled worker placed it seventh. Here again, Maslow may come into play: The unskilled worker is more likely than his skilled counterpart to find himself in an unsatisfactory physical environment (unfulfilled need).

Organizational Level

The organizational levels were divided into lower, middle, and higher nonsupervisory categories. The comparison of the lower with both the middle and the higher levels produced statistically significant differences.

The greatest difference was that the lower organization level employees rated "good wages" first and "job security" second, whereas both the middle and the higher levels rated "interesting work" first and "full appreciation of work done" second. Here is more evidence that basic needs must be satisfied before the higher needs are expressed.

MANIPULATING THE REWARD SYSTEM

According to all three surveys, supervisors feel that money is the major motivator of their employees. But only three of the employee subgroups rated money as the most important reward. These subgroups were as follows:

- The under–30 group, representing 20 percent of the total survey
- The under-$12,000 income level, representing 13.5 percent of the total
- The lower organization level employee, representing 42 percent of the total survey

Why do managers choose to ignore the reward responses made by most of the workers under their supervision? Managers seem to operate under a self-reference system; they rank rewards as they would want them for themselves and assume that their employees would subscribe to the same rewards.

If this *is* true—and the survey results confirm that it is true—then how can management be encouraged to base employee policies on more objective interpretations of employee motivations?

One way to encourage more objectivity in structuring reward systems is to do attitude surveys such as this one. This survey revealed that supervisors do not know what their employees want. It also revealed differences among employee subgroups that management should take into consideration when structuring reward systems.

Managers need to be aware that reward practices should be designed to fit the needs of particular people working under particular conditions. Using the current survey as an example, how can reward systems be manipulated for the various groupings?

Male/Female

According to this survey, men are more inclined to prefer interesting work, whereas women need more appreciation of work well done. Efforts should be made to design interesting jobs—both groups marked "interesting work" as one of the three primary rewards. But managers who take into account the fact that women workers have more need of appreciation will engage in verbal communication intended to foster such a feeling.

Age Group

Flexible pay incentives might be used effectively with the under–30 workers who are concerned about their basic needs. Older groups can be expected to respond more positively to job enrichment and job enlargement programs.

The 41–50 group gave first place to the "feeling of being in on things." Systems of top-down vertical communication within the organization would appear to be particularly effective with this group. Supervisors who deal with the 41–50 age group might well make an effort to include this group in discussions of policy, even if their ideas are not always implemented.

The over–50 group places moderate importance on "good working conditions," "personal loyalty to employees," and "sympathetic help with personal problems." A manager who is aware of these needs can help these employees be more productive.

Income

Lower-income employees, who are primarily concerned with "good wages," would respond well to pay incentive programs. They are moderately concerned with "full appreciation of work done," "interesting work," and the "feeling of being in on things." All of the other income groups are primarily concerned with "interesting work" and "full appreciation of work done."

A job enrichment/job enlargement program would probably work for all income groups except the lowest one, whereas an incentive pay program (for example, piece-rate or the Scanlon plan) might motivate lower income employees.

Job Types

The most striking difference between the unskilled blue-collar worker and the unskilled white-collar worker is the emphasis placed on "good working conditions." The unskilled white-collar workers, who put this second on their list of preferences, were the only group to give this factor so high a rating. Supervisors of this group should be able to address the physical working conditions by a simple environmental analysis and reap some motivational return.

The difference between blue-collar skilled and white-collar skilled workers is significant in the positioning of "full appreciation of work done." Skilled blue-collar workers evidently have a high self-awareness of how well they do their jobs, whereas white-collar workers need outside confirmation of job worth.

Because of their need to be in on things, blue-collar skilled workers should be included in more decision-making activities. Skilled white-collar workers respond well to the same stimuli as their blue-collar counterparts but for a different reason. Greater participation in decision-making activities provides these white-collar workers with the feedback they need to define their jobs and better opportunities to receive the exposure needed for advancement.

Organizational Level

Employees at the lower organizational level would respond to pay incentives and greater job security. In the middle and higher levels employees respond to job enrichment and job enlargement programs.

In the middle organizational level, respondents assigned job security the number four position, the same position as the total respondent ranking. Management should seriously consider the insecurity experienced by workers in the industrial sector.

Evidently job security matters to people who don't have it, as evidenced by the under–30 group giving it second position, the 31–40 group (a group that may find it more difficult to change jobs) ranking it first, and the over–50 group (the group with the most security) ranking it seventh. The higher organizational level group, probably those with the most security, placed job security in the number six position. Again, the evidence supports Maslow's contention that fulfilled needs no longer motivate.

THE IMPORTANCE OF ATTITUDE SURVEYS

With the exception of two groups—the group under 30 and the group making less than $12,000 a year—all of the respondents ranked "interesting work" in one of the three top positions.

For thirty years a large utility company asked job applicants to rank-order ten job characteristics in terms of their importance to the applicants. A study that drew on this experience came up with results similar to those shown in Table 2.[6] Over this thirty-year period, job security declined in importance and "type of work" increased in importance. Furthermore, when the respondents were grouped according to educational attainment, people with higher education attached more importance to type of work, whereas those with only high school diplomas attached more importance to job security.

Because each year the American labor force contains a higher percentage of people with postsecondary education, the importance of interesting work will increase.

Making work interesting is not an easy task, however. It is much easier to pay more, to make work cleaner and safer, even to ensure reasonable job security than it is to make some kinds of work interesting. Perhaps in the future job enlargement and enrichment need to be tried on a far larger scale than has been done in the past. Surely the work of Frederick Herzberg would support such a notion. Organizations with considerable numbers of younger, lower-paid workers may well take a long look at these behavioral concepts.

Many studies in the field of job satisfaction are in general agreement that most workers are satisfied with their jobs. Workers between 20 and 29, however, are the least satisfied. A study of this particular group found that 24 percent—almost one in four—held negative attitudes toward their work.[7]

Job satisfaction is a difficult thing to measure. It is tied to the expectations of the workers who answer the question, and it is difficult to evaluate against a fixed scale of intensity. At what point, for example, do a person's cumulative negative feelings add up to an overall assessment that he or she is dissatisfied with a given job? Only the individual person can make such a judgment.

This does not mean that we cannot generalize from these surveys. For example, it appears that, in most cases, the basic needs of the worker are met by industrial organizations. That is, wages are not a burning issue except with those under age 30 earning less than $12,000 a year, and at the lowest organizational level.

What most employees consider important is "interesting work," "appreciation of work," and the "feeling of being in on things." Supervisors should be aware of the importance of these particular values and encourage upper-level management to restructure jobs and construct better communications within the organization. They should be aware that the employees want to be appreciated and should make an effort to give credit where credit is due. Whenever possible, they should include all levels of employees in some forms of decision making, so that employees have a feeling of belonging and participating.

Surveys of attitudes enable supervisors to spot potential dissatisfaction factors that could arise because of changes in the makeup of the work force and in the background of the employees. And frequent surveys help to impress on managers their responsibility to take into account the needs of employees.

To know what are the specific needs of employees, attitude surveys are necessary. Because of today's rapidly changing society, these surveys need to be taken often. Self-reference, a major problem in employee motivation for at least forty years, will not and cannot be eliminated or even minimized any other way.

The High-Wage Myth

The results of attitude surveys should be disseminated to the supervisors directly in charge of the employees, not held in the hands of upper-level management. These results may help to dispel the notion held by supervisors that their employees are motivated by high wages above everything else, even though this false notion has been disproved by practically every study over forty years. In 1963 Saul W. Gellerman stated: "Myths die hard. It is quite clear that money's reputation as the ultimate motivation is going to be a long time a-dying."[8]

As the current survey shows, this myth is still alive and flourishing. Most supervisors in the industrial sector still believe it.

Maslow contended that under current business conditions, most American employees have lower-level or deficit needs substantially satisfied. Therefore, such management strategies as increasing employee incomes or strengthening job security will not accomplish as much as often expected.

The results of these surveys bear out Maslow's contention, but they point out that there exists a class of employees whose basic needs still are not satisfied. The surveys show the degree to which various respondents' job circumstances provide sufficient rewards in each job area. If today's industrial organizations were to administer a similar survey, it would be a giant first step toward improving employee motivation in the United States.

MOTIVATION AND PRODUCTIVITY

In his book *Reality-Centered People Management*, Erwin S. Stanton states: "The most worrisome problem facing American business today is that of low employee work productivity."[9]

Historically, America's industrial gains have been the highest in the world, but lately our productivity growth has declined, particularly when compared with some of our industrial competitors. In 1986 the United States, along with Great Britain, had the lowest rate of productivity gains in the past ten years, a cumulative 27 percent. In the same period Japan gained 107 percent and West Germany 70 percent.[10] The decline in employee motivation and in commitment to high-quality work performance may well be one of the major causes of this productivity slowdown.

What is needed is a management style that is flexible, that takes into account the types of employees being supervised, recognizing their differing abilities and diverse motivational needs. What is being advocated is theory Y style of management that takes everyone's needs into account as much as is consistent with the requirements of the production schedule.

A decline in productivity is a cost that many companies cannot afford and that the United States, with its high standard of living, cannot tolerate. Increasing foreign competition already has caused many of our corporations serious problems and failures.

Proper motivation of employees is directly associated with productivity (a direct cost) and with maintenance factors (an indirect cost). Workers who are content with their jobs, who feel challenged, who have the opportunity to fulfill their goals will exhibit less destructive behavior on the job. They will be absent less frequently, they will be less inclined to change jobs, and, most important, they will produce at a higher level.

Management must understand what motivates employees within the context of the roles they perform. Such an understanding is crucial to improved productivity and, ultimately, to the health of our industry and our nation as a whole. Surveys are not a cure-all. But if companies periodically administer them and take to heart their results, incorporating them whenever possible in manipulating the reward system, employees, supervisors, the company, and the country stand to gain a great deal.

NOTES

1. Kenneth A. Kovach, "Why Motivational Theories Don't Work," *Society for the Advancement of Management Advanced Management Journal*, Spring 1980, p. 56.

2. Abraham H. Maslow, "A Theory of Human Motivation," *Psychological Review*, July 1943, pp. 370–96.

3. Frederick Herzberg, Bernard Mausner, and Barbara Block Snyderman, *The Motivation to Work* (New York: John Wiley & Sons, 1959).

4. See Alan C. Filley and Robert J. House, "Some Empirical Evidence about Needs Theory," in *Managerial Motivation and Compensation* (Ann Arbor: University of Michigan, 1972), p. 239.

5. David C. McClelland, "The Role of Money in Managing Motivation," *Managerial Motivation and Compensation* (Ann Arbor: University of Michigan, 1972), p. 527.

6. C. E. Jurgensen, "Job Preferences: What Makes a Job Good or Bad?" *Journal of Applied Psychology*, 63 (June 1978), pp. 267–76.

7. H. L. Sheppard and N. Q. Herrick, *Where Have All the Robots Gone?* (New York: Free Press, 1972).

8. S. W. Gellerman, *Motivation and Productivity* (New York: AMA, 1963), p. 64.

9. Erwin S. Stanton, *Reality-Centered People Management* (New York: AMA-COM, 1982), p. v.

10. See Raj Aggarwal, "The Strategic Challenge of the Evolving Global Economy," *Business Horizons* 30 (July-August 1987), pp. 38–44.

Do's and Don'ts in Dealing with Employee Theft

James P. McElligott, Jr.

A. To reduce problems from employee theft, an employer should do the following:

1. Do have a thorough control system to trace the handling and disposition of merchandise, cash, and items convertible into cash.

2. Do review your control system from time to time to find weak points that may leave you vulnerable to theft and embezzlement.

3. Do have an experienced "embezzlement/theft team" to investigate and act on suspected incidents of theft or embezzlement.

4. Do know applicable state and federal laws regulating polygraph (i.e., Federal Employee Polygraph Protection Act of 1988) and other screening devices.

5. Do ask applicants about any criminal convictions.

6. Do consider seeking a criminal history record request from the state police.

7. Do keep information on arrests, charges, or convictions strictly confidential.

8. Do verify facts thoroughly before taking any adverse action based on any prior criminal record.

9. Do treat suspected incidents consistently, without favoritism or special treatment to any person or group.

10. Do know the ground rules in your collective bargaining agree-

ment and/or personnel policies as they apply to the employee theft/embezzlement situation.

11. Do remember that prosecuting employee theft or embezzlement will require proof beyond a reasonable doubt.

12. Do conduct an immediate and thorough investigation.

13. Do preserve original documents and physical evidence to prevent loss or alteration.

14. Do instruct all people questioned, and all people who learn of the investigation, that the investigation is strictly confidential.

15. Do remember, and instruct all concerned to remember, that the confidentiality instruction was given.

16. Do keep an open mind until proof beyond a reasonable doubt is obtained.

17. Do treat all people interrogated in a professional, nonaccusatory manner—especially the suspect.

18. Do be patient and thorough when interrogating suspects—get the minute details and check them out.

19. Do advise employees in employment applications and personnel handbooks if you expect them to be subject to periodic searches.

20. Do obtain consent, in writing or in the presence of other witnesses, before searching any employee unless you know and follow the rules under which non-consensual searches may be made.

21. Do obtain an admission of theft or embezzlement in writing as soon as the suspect confesses.

22. Do insist on immediate restitution.

23. Do keep in mind that the thief or embezzler has almost certainly stolen or embezzled more than he has confessed.

24. Do consult legal counsel before firing an employee for theft.

25. Do consult legal counsel before pressing criminal charges.

26. Do assume that you will have to take the lead in proving the theft or embezzlement.

27. Do keep restitution totally separate from the decision to press charges.

28. Do review your fidelity bond and give appropriate notice to your bonding company.

29. Do review your operations after any incident of suspected theft,

and make appropriate revisions to your control and/or operating system.

B. To avoid legal problems arising from investigation of employee theft, an employer should *not* do the following:

1. Act on assumption or secondhand information.

2. Tell an employee he is being fired for theft unless you are prepared to prove the theft beyond a reasonable doubt.

3. Press charges against a former employee unless you are prepared to prove those charges beyond a reasonable doubt.

4. As a general rule, fire an employee suspected of theft without first conducting a thorough investigation, including careful interrogation of the employee in an attempt to obtain a confession.

5. Expect an employee to confess theft or embezzlement when first confronted with incriminating evidence.

6. Ask employees about prior arrests or make decisions based on arrest records.

7. Promise or suggest that you will not prosecute if the employee makes restitution.

8. Assume that the police or prosecutor will properly investigate or prosecute any charges you press.

9. Use polygraphs without following the detailed requirements of the Federal Employee Polygraph Protection Act of 1988 and any applicable state laws.

10. Disclose facts concerning an employee's misconduct or suspected misconduct unless the person to whom you reveal it has a clear need to know and you are prepared to prove the truth of what you disclose.

Copyright © by permission James P. McElligott, Jr., "Do's and Don't's In Dealing with Employee Theft."

Internal Controls Checklist

Neil H. Snyder, O. Whitfield Broome, Jr., and Karen Zimmerman

GENERAL

1. Is the general accounting function completely separated from:
   a. Cash receipts and disbursements?
   b. Sales?
   c. Purchasing?
   d. Manufacturing?
   e. Inventory management?
2. Are employees who handle cash and securities bonded?
3. Are all such employees required to take annual vacations?
4. Are their duties assigned to others during the vacation period?
5. Are journal entries approved by a person other than the one preparing the entries?
6. Do journal entries contain adequate explanations?
7. Are monthly financial statements prepared for the management?
   a. Are they compared with the budget?
   b. Are they compared with the prior year?
8. Is there a current organizational chart?
9. Are the accounting and treasury functions satisfactorily defined and segregated?
10. To whom does the chief accounting officer report?
11. Does the company have:
    a. An internal auditor?
    b. Someone to whom he reports?

12. Is a chart of accounts used? Does it contain descriptions of the types of entries affecting each account?

13. Is there an accounting manual in current use?

14. Are costs and expenses under budgetary control?

15. Is insurance coverage for major items such as inventory, property, plant and equipment, and public liability reviewed periodically by a responsible officer for adequacy?

16. Does an officer or a responsible employee maintain a calendar or tickler file relating to the due dates of tax returns and special reports, the expiration dates of the statute of limitations on tax refund claims, etc.?

17. What is the company's policy with respect to its officers and key employees having any direct or indirect ownership or profit participation in outside businesses with which the company does business? What procedures are followed to determine that such policy is being complied with?

18. Has last year's management letter been reviewed to determine whether all recommendations were implemented?

19. Are the books of account adequate for the business?

20. Does the client have a controller?

21. Are the duties of employees rotated in the accounting department?

22. Are any members of the accounting department related to other members of the department?

23. Are any relatives of the accounting department staff employed by the company?

24. Are all entries in the books of account supported by books of original entry or journal entry?

25. Are all entries in the books of accounts supported by a document that gave rise to the transaction?

26. Are there any bank accounts in the name of the corporation not on the books of account?

27. Are summary totals of journal columns checked monthly?

28. Is the pension or retirement plan administered by a trustee?

CASH

1. Are all bank accounts authorized by the board of directors?

2. Is there a list of how many bank accounts are maintained and what the purpose of each account is?

3. If there are any inactive bank accounts, is there an explanation of why they are maintained?

CASH RECEIPTS

1. Is the receipt of currency, as opposed to checks and drafts, insignificant?

2. Are cash receipts provable by cash register tapes, counter sales slips, collector's receipts, etc.?

3. Are these proofs checked by an employee independent of the one receiving cash, preparing deposits, or recording cash receipts?

4. Are change funds provided?

5. Regarding mail:
   a. Is mail opened by a person who has no access to cash receipts records?
   b. Are mail receipts listed by a person who has no access to cash receipts records?

6. Is this listing of mail receipts subsequently compared with the cash receipts records by a person who has no access to cash?

7. Regarding daily receipts:
   a. Are each day's receipts deposited intact promptly?
   b. Does the company forbid the cashing of checks from daily receipts?

8. Does someone other than the person recording cash receipts prepare the deposits?

9. Are the duties of this person such that he or she has no access to the customers' ledgers and monthly statements?

10. Is an authenticated duplicate deposit slip received by someone other than the people receiving cash, making the deposit, and recording cash receipts?

11. Does this person compare such authenticated duplicate deposit slips with:
    a. The record of incoming remittances?
    b. The cash book entries?

12. Are specific people responsible for receipts from the time cash is received until it is deposited?

13. Are postdated checks safeguarded against loss?

14. Are all people who are responsible for cash receipts bonded?

15. Has the client's bank been instructed not to cash checks payable to the company?

16. If the names of customers are not readily determinable on remittances, are they deposited without delay?

17. Where branch offices make collections, are such collections deposited immediately in a local bank account subject only to home office withdrawals?

18. Is independent accounting control established outside the cashier's department over miscellaneous receipts, rent, interest, cash sales, sales of scrap, etc.?

19. Are surprise audits of cash receipts made periodically?

20. Are checks returned by the bank followed up for subsequent disposition?

21. Are bank advices for debits, credits, and uncollectible checks received by a person other than the one who has responsibility for handling cash receipts?

22. If receipts are issued, are they prenumbered?

23. Is a permanent copy of an issued receipt maintained in a book?

24. Is it reviewed for alteration?

25. For receipts over the counter, are prenumbered invoices prepared?

26. If outside salespeople or routepeople receive money from a customer:

    a. Is accountability maintained over the merchandise that they have in their possession?

    b. Are their reports reviewed by a responsible executive of the company?

27. Are checks restrictively endorsed immediately?

28. Are customer remittance advices, rather than the checks, forwarded to accounts receivable for crediting to customers' accounts?

CASH DISBURSEMENTS

1. Are checks prenumbered and accounted for?

2. Are blank checks adequately safeguarded and under the control of people who do not prepare checks?

3. Are voided checks mutilated, kept, and filed?

4. Is the person preparing checks independent of purchasing, receiving, and inventory functions?

5. Is a check protector used?

6. Are all payments (other than from petty cash) made by check?

7. Are authorized signatures limited to employees who have no access to:

    a. Accounting records?

    b. Cash receipts?

    c. Petty cash funds?

    d. Bank reconciliations?

8. Are checks countersigned?

9. Is the signing or countersigning of checks in advance prohibited?

10. a. Is the practice of drawing checks to cash or bearer prohibited?

    b. Is the use of counter checks forbidden?

11. Do supporting documents accompany checks submitted for signature?

12. Do supporting documents include evidence of receipt and approval?

13. Are supporting documents effectively canceled to prevent subsequent misuse?

14. Are the check signers designated by the board of directors?

15. What procedures have been adopted to ensure that people who are no longer

authorized to sign checks are removed from the authorized list maintained at the banks?

16. When a mechanical check signer is used, is the signature dye under adequate control?

17. Are there limitations on the amounts of single-signature checks?

18. Is a control book over the number of signature impressions in use?

19. Are checks ever signed in blank?

20. Are people who sign checks or control the use of facsimile signature plates independent of those:

    a. Requesting the expenditure?

    b. Approving the expenditure?

    c. Reconciling the bank account?

    d. Preparing the check?

21. Is the checkbook balanced, maintained, and in agreement with the general ledger balance?

22. Are stale checks outstanding automatically canceled with the bank?

PETTY CASH

1. Are petty cash disbursements approved by a responsible official?

2. Are petty cash disbursements adequately supported?

3. Is the imprest or I.O.U. system used?

4. Are cash receipts segregated from the petty cash fund?

5. Is responsibility for each fund vested in only one person?

6. Are petty cash vouchers marked paid to prevent duplicate payment?

7. Are checks cashed from the fund only when made payable to the custodian?

8. a. Are wage and salary advances made from the fund?

    b. If so, are the same approvals required as for advances made by check?

9. Is the dollar volume of petty cash transactions reasonable?

10. Is access to the fund denied to all employees other than the custodian?

11. Is the fund periodically counted by someone other than the custodian?

12. Are vouchers submitted for reimbursement approved by a responsible person?

13. Are vouchers reviewed by someone other than the one approving them at the time of reimbursement of the fund?

14. Are vouchers filled out in ink?

15. Are vouchers prenumbered?

16. Are receipts attached to the vouchers supporting the request for reimbursement?

17. Are personal checks of employees cashed by the custodian of the fund?

18. Are personal checks cashed by the custodian held for long periods of time?
19. Are payroll checks cashed by the custodian of the fund?
20. Is the fund reimbursed less frequently than weekly?
21. Is the fund periodically counted on a surprise basis?
22. Are maximum expenditure amounts set for petty cash?

BANK RECONCILIATIONS

1. Are monthly bank reconciliations prepared by an employee other than one who has access to cash, signs checks, or records cash transactions?
2. Does that employee receive the bank statements unopened?
3. Does that employee examine paid checks for dates, payees, cancellations and endorsements, account for numerical sequence, etc.?
4. With respect to checks outstanding for an undue period of time:

    a. Are such checks investigated?

    b. Is payment stopped and an entry made to restore such items to cash?
5. Are bank reconciliations reviewed critically each month by an officer or responsible employee?
6. Are canceled checks compared with the disbursements journal as to amount, date, and payee?
7. Are the dates and amounts of deposits on bank statements compared with the cash receipts journal?
8. Are interbank transfers investigated to determine that both sides of the transaction have been recorded?

SALES, SHIPPING, AND BILLING

1. Are all sales checked for the customer's credit standing before the order is filled?
2. Are sales invoices prenumbered and accounted for?
3. Are shipping documents prenumbered?
4. Are shipping documents independently checked with sales invoices to assure that all shipments are billed?
5. Are customers required to furnish a purchase order?
6. Are sales invoices checked for accuracy of:

    a. Quantities billed?

    b. Prices used?

    c. Extensions and additions?

    d. Terms?
7. Is the entry and numerical sequence of sales invoices independently checked?

8. Do employees of the shipping department have access to the stockrooms?

9. Is the billing department entirely separate from the accounts receivable and shipping departments?

10. Are confirmations of orders regularly sent to customers?

11. Does the billing department receive directly from the shipping department a record of all shipments made, and from the purchasing or accounts payable department a record of items shipped directly to customers from suppliers?

12. Are prices for merchandise shipped obtained from a standard price list?

13. Are exceptions to standard pricing approved in writing by a member of the sales department?

14. Are variations from standard prices approved by an executive outside of the sales department?

15. Does the accounts receivable department receive a copy of all invoices directly from the billing department?

16. Are voided invoices initiated by a supervisor and retained in numerical sequence?

17. Are daily sales totaled, recorded by the billing department, and reconciled with the total amount posted to the customers' accounts each day?

18. Are pro forma billings, consignments, and shipments to outside processors excluded from sales?

19. Are credit memos for goods returned correlated with receiving slips?

20. Are freight allowances made to customers controlled, including the requirement that paid freight bills be submitted by customers?

21. Are the shipping and billing departments prohibited from handling company funds?

22. Are special orders authorized by appropriate officials?

23. Are shipments checked against the order for correctness of quantity, model, etc.?

24. Are shipping documents prepared by someone independent of the shipping department?

25. Are C.O.D. shipments treated like regular credit sales?

ACCOUNTS RECEIVABLE

1. Are customers' ledgers balanced regularly with the general ledger controlling account?

2. Are monthly statements sent to all customers?

3. Are monthly statements independently checked to the accounts, and controlled and mailed by someone other than the accounts receivable bookkeeper?

4. Are the accounts aged periodically?

   a. Are the aged trial balances reviewed by a responsible official?

5. Are delinquent accounts reviewed by a responsible official?

6. Is there a regular prescribed series of collection letters for use with slow-payment customers?

7. Are disputed items handled by someone other than the accounts receivable bookkeeper?

8. Are write-offs of bad debts authorized by a responsible official?

9. Are credit memoranda approved by proper authority?

10. Are credit memoranda under numerical control?

11. Are the duties of the accounts receivable bookkeeper completely separate from any cash and credit functions?

12. Is the selling function kept separate from the delivery or shipping function?

13. Are general ledger entries made by an employee other than the accounts receivable bookkeeper?

14. Are discounts taken checked by an officer or responsible employee?

15. Is adequate control exercised over bad accounts previously written off?

16. Is control over sales returns (both accounts receivable and inventory) adequate?

    a. Are such credits to customers' accounts approved by a responsible official?

17. Are the receivable bookkeepers rotated among various ledgers from time to time?

18. Are entries to accounts reflecting advances to employees reviewed by an authorized employee independent of the one who keeps the accounts?

19. With respect to customer credit balances:

    a. Are customers advised of credit balances in their accounts?

    b. Is approval of the credit department required before payment of customer credit balances?

20. Are adequate controls maintained over miscellaneous receivables for:

    a. Freight and insurance claims?

    b. Sales of scrap?

    c. Sales of equipment?

    d. Rental and miscellaneous income?

    e. Interest?

    f. Tax refunds?

21. Are cutoff procedures adequate at closing periods?

22. Is the customer's account ever charged before the merchandise is delivered?

23. Are credit limits reviewed by a responsible official?

24. Are claims by customers for damage or short shipments recorded on the books of account as they arise?

    a. Is effective follow-up and disposition of these items made?

25. Are accounts periodically confirmed?

26. Are accounts written off controlled for follow-up and possible subsequent collection?

NOTES RECEIVABLE

1. Are notes and renewals authorized by a responsible official?

2. Is the custodian of notes independent of employees receiving cash or recording transactions?

3. Is collateral, if any, adequately controlled?

4. Are partial payments endorsed on the back of notes?

5. Is an account maintained for notes receivable discounted?

6. Are write-offs on notes approved by an officer?

7. Are dishonored notes followed up for subsequent collection?

8. Is compliance with credit terms reviewed independently?

INVESTMENTS

1. Are securities kept under lock and key or in a safety deposit box?

2. Is it necessary for more than one person to be present to open the safety deposit box, and are such people independent of record keeping?

3. Are signatures required for access to securities and are reports of all such access required?

4. Are securities examined by responsible officials periodically and reconciled with the controlling accounts?

5. Is a record kept of each security, including certificate numbers?

6. Are securities registered in the name of the company?

7. Are purchases and sales of securities authorized by:

    a. A responsible officer?

    b. The board of directors?

8. Is income from notes and investments accounted for periodically?

9. Is approval of an officer required for write-off of worthless investments, the release of collateral, and the receipt and delivery of securities?

10. Are investments that are written off renewed periodically as to possible realization?

11. If securities are held by a custodian, is confirmation of those held regularly obtained?

INVENTORIES

A. *General*

1. Is the custodian of the inventory independent of purchasing and receiving functions?

2. Are properly authorized, receipted requisitions required for all withdrawals from storerooms?

3. Is access to the stockroom or warehouse controlled?

4. Are goods kept in order?

5. Is adequate control maintained over material in the hands of suppliers or processors?

6. Are aged schedules of inventory prepared and reviewed by responsible officials?

7. Are all inventory classes physically counted during the year?

8. Are inventories off premises confirmed or physically counted during the year?

9. Are prenumbered tags used in counting of physical inventories?

10. Are items in physical inventories counted by one employee and rechecked by another?

11. Are receiving reports independently prepared?

12. Do storekeepers compare quantities received with production reports?

13. Is there adequate control over the accumulation and sale of scrap?

B. *Perpetual Inventory Systems*

14. Are perpetual inventory records maintained?

15. Are the perpetual inventory records controlled by the general books?

16. Is the custodian of the inventory a person other than the one keeping the inventory books?

17. Are the perpetual inventory records periodically checked with merchandise in stock?

    a. Is this done by persons independent of those keeping the inventory records?

    b. Is there written approval by a responsible employee of adjustments made to perpetual records based on physical inventories?

C. *Retail Inventory Systems*

18. Are periodic physical inventories taken at retail and compared in total with the retail inventory records?

19. Are retail price changes supported by written authorizations?

D. *Year-End Inventory*

20. Are written instructions regarding year-end inventories prepared for the guidance of participating employees?

21. Is a definite policy in effect regarding the inventorying of obsolete merchandise?

22. Are year-end inventories taken under the supervision of responsible officials?

23. Are the following steps pertaining to year-end inventories double-checked:

    a. Quantity determination?

    b. Summarizations of quantities?

    c. Pricing?

    d. Extension and additions?

    e. Summarizations of detailed inventory sheets?

24. Is merchandise on hand that is not the property of the client physically segregated and under accounting control?

25. Is proper control exercised over obsolete and slow-moving goods and materials?

E. Other

26. Are inventories that are stored in public warehouses physically checked from time to time?

27. Does the basis of pricing inventory give proper consideration to all direct and indirect elements of cost?

28. Are procedures in effect to ensure proper cutoffs at inventory dates?

29. Are significant overages and shortages carefully investigated?

PROPERTY, PLANT, AND EQUIPMENT

1. Does the client maintain detailed subsidiary records of property, plant, and equipment and of accumulated depreciation?

    a. Are detailed fixed asset records maintained for each item?

    b. Do the records indicate the year of acquisition, the cost, the method of depreciation, and the accumulated depreciation to date?

2. Are such detailed records kept in balance with the control accounts?

3. Are capital expenditures authorized by responsible officials?

4. Is there a written policy for distinguishing between capital expenditures and maintenance and repair items?

5. Is accounting control maintained on retirements and sales?

6. Are periodic checks made of the physical existence by comparison of the items shown in the detail records with those in service?

7. Is there adequate control over the continued use of fully depreciated assets?

8. Are depreciation rates reviewed periodically to determine if there is any unforeseen obsolescence?

9. Are actual expenditures for fixed assets compared with approved and authorized estimates?

10. Are physical inventories taken of small tools and movable equipment?

11. Is control maintained over the status of property (e.g., moving, sales, scrapping) and are the records adjusted for these changes?

12. Are items of property identified by number?

13. If fixed assets are regularly constructed by the company, are expenses incurred in connection with such construction properly segregated and capitalized?

PURCHASING AND RECEIVING

1. Is the responsibility for purchasing assigned to one person?
    a. Is this person independent of receiving and disbursing functions?
2. Are all purchase orders:
    a. Prenumbered and controlled?
    b. Required for all purchases except services?
    c. Prepared on the basis of purchase requisitions or, where applicable, production schedules prepared by other departments?
    d. Approved by a responsible employee in the department preparing the requisitions?
3. Is the responsibility for receiving incoming merchandise assigned to one person?
    a. Is this person independent of purchasing and disbursing?
4. Are prenumbered receiving tickets used for all incoming merchandise?
    a. Are they signed, dated, prenumbered, and controlled?
5. Is a numerical file or similar record of receiving tickets maintained?
6. Are invoice prices, extensions, and additions checked?
7. Are freight charges checked?
8. Are expenditures for major services approved by the board of directors?
9. Is the client taking advantage of all available discounts?
10. Does a responsible employee establish the distribution of purchase and expense items?
11. Are competitive bids obtained on purchase of materials, supplies, and services, including construction contracts, over specified minimum amounts?
12. Do the records indicate why purchases were not made from the lowest bidder, if such is the case?
13. Does the company have a list of vendors and suppliers that have been approved in accordance with company policy?
14. Does a responsible person review the prices paid for items to determine that such prices are not in excess of market?
15. With respect to the acceptance by employees of gifts or other gratuities from vendors:
    a. Does the company have a policy on this?
    b. Is this policy made known to vendors in writing from time to time?
16. Are cutoff procedures adequate at closing periods?
17. Do purchase orders above prescribed limits require approval by someone other than the buyer?
18. Do purchase orders indicate the account distribution?

19. Are copies of the purchase order distributed to:
    a. The receiving department?
    b. The accounting department?
20. Are the accounting department and other departments notified with respect to:
    a. Direct shipments from the vendor to a customer?
    b. Direct shipments from the vendor to a subcontractor?
    c. Shipments from the vendor to a public warehouse?
21. Is an adequate record kept of incomplete purchase orders?
22. Are schedules of long-term contracts maintained?
23. Do commitments for materials extend beyond the normal operating cycle?
    a. Are they approved by a responsible person?
24. Is all incoming merchandise, materials, and supplies required to pass through a single receiving point, stage, plant, or location?
25. Are merchandise, materials, and supplies inspected for condition, and counted, weighed, or measured in the receiving department?
26. If copies of the purchase order are supplied to the personnel in the receiving department, are quantities omitted to require an independent, actual count of quantities received?
27. Are copies of receiving slips and all receiving records sent to:
    a. Accounts payable?
    b. The inventory department?
    c. The buyers?
28. Are shortages, rejections, and damage claims immediately reported?

ACCOUNTS PAYABLE

1. Is a voucher or purchase register maintained?
2. Is an accounts payable subsidiary ledger maintained?
3. Is the accounts payable subsidiary ledger balanced with the general ledger controlling account regularly?
4. Are suppliers' monthly statements regularly compared with recorded liabilities?
5. Is control of creditors' invoices immediately established on receipt?
6. With respect to partial shipments from vendors:
    a. Is control clearly maintained, indicating on the purchase order information as to the payment thereof, to avoid duplicate payment on completion of the order?
    b. Are there any other procedures in effect to prevent duplicate payments on partial shipment by vendors?
7. Are duplicate copies of invoices marked immediately on receipt to prevent duplicate payments?
8. Does processing of the items for payment include:
    a. Check of terms, prices, and quantities on invoices against purchase orders?
    b. Check of items and quantities on invoices against the reports obtained directly from the receiving department?
    c. Mathematical check of quotings, extensions, and discounts?
    d. Indication of account distribution?

  e. Review of invoices for items unsupported by purchase orders for approval by department heads?

  f. Indication on the voucher that all checks and approvals above have been made?

9. Are vendor's invoices altered?

10. Are debit memos issued to vendors instead of changing the amounts and quantities?

11. Are discounts indicated on the invoice at the time of receipt?

12. Are prepayments or deposits with vendors maintained under control and applied when paying the related invoices?

13. With respect to travel and entertainment, is accounting for expenditures sufficient evidence as required by the Internal Revenue Code?

14. When payments for services rendered are made directly to customers by vendors, are procedures adequate to ensure that the related receivables and payables are recorded within the same accounting period?

15. Are return purchases controlled in a manner that ensures that the vendors will be charged therefor?

16. Are unmatched purchase orders and receiving reports periodically investigated?

17. On disputed items, are the amounts entered on the books of account and the invoice maintained in separate files?

18. Are the people working in accounts payable a different group from those working on cash receipts and the preparation and mailing of checks?

19. Is there a system of cross-referencing from voucher to check in the event a voucher system is used?

20. Are debit balances in accounts payable periodically reviewed for requests for reimbursements by vendors?

21. Are all invoices or vouchers reviewed and approved by a responsible executive other than the one who initiated the purchase?

PAYROLL

1. Are written authorizations for new employees and changes in salary or wage rates on file?

2. Is the time of hourly employees that appears on payrolls supported by approved time cards?

3. Are salaries and wages paid by check?

4. Are payroll disbursements made from a special bank account restricted to that purpose?

5. Are payroll checks signed by employees who do not participate in:
  a. Preparation of the payroll?
  b. Handling of cash funds?
  c. Maintenance of accounting records?

6. Are payroll computations independently checked?

7. If the payroll is paid in cash:
  a. Is the person distributing the cash someone other than the person preparing the payroll?
  b. Are signed receipts obtained from employees?

c. Are such pay receipts promptly canceled after proof against disbursements, to prevent reuse?

8. Are unclaimed wages adequately controlled?

9. Are adequate payroll records maintained for:
   a. Individual payroll cards?
   b. Departmental payroll sheets?

10. Are mechanical time clocks used for hourly employees?

11. Are the duties of those preparing the payroll rotated?

12. Are the people who perform the following functions independent of one another?
    a. Approve hours worked
    b. Prepare the payroll
    c. Distribute the pay
    d. Maintain custody of unclaimed wages

13. Is there a separate personnel department that maintains complete personnel records, including wage and salary data?

14. Are authorizations signed by employees required for other than compulsory deductions from taxes?

15. Are there adequate procedures to assure correct time-reporting, such as:
    a. Use of time clocks?
    b. Independent timekeepers?
    c. Production reports?
    d. Attendance of salaried employees?
    e. Piecework reporting?

16. Are written approvals obtained for:
    a. Alterations of time cards?
    b. Failure to punch in and out?
    c. Overtime work?
    d. Paid absences or sick leave?

17. Are company policy manuals in effect to cover for salaried employees:
    a. Paid holidays?
    b. Vacation pay?
    c. Sick leave?
    d. Time off?

18. Are labor distribution tickets independently computed and tabulated to provide an independent check on aggregate pay?

19. Are payrolls subject to review and final approval by responsible people outside the payroll department, such as department heads, foremen, and controllers?

20. In reconciliation, are checks compared with payroll records and endorsements scrutinized?

21. Are departmental distributions for salaries and wages carefully made, and checked and approved by an accounting official?

22. Are periodic audits of payrolls made?

23. Do periodic audits include witnessing of distribution of paychecks or envelopes to identify each person and an accounting made of those not immediately distributed?

24. If incentive wage systems are used, is production reporting periodically checked independently to production or sales data?
25. If incentive wage systems are used, are standards periodically reviewed to compare them with time wage rates, and are fluctuations between the two reviewed to create action?

NOTES PAYABLE AND LONG-TERM DEBT

1. Do resolutions of the board of directors authorize borrowings and specifically delineate those officers empowered to borrow on behalf of the corporation?
2. Are notes payable registers maintained, indicating the maturity date and amount of the note?
3. Are the registers periodically balanced with the general ledger?
4. Are schedules of interest earned on debt discount prepared regularly?
5. Are redeemed notes maintained in the company's files?
6. Does the company regularly ascertain that restrictions contained in the debt agreements are being complied with?
7. Are adequate records maintained to determine assets collateralizing indebtedness?

CAPITAL STOCK

1. Are unissued stock certificates prenumbered and maintained under security conditions?
2. Is a stockholders' ledger maintained for each class of authorized and outstanding capital stock, indicating the name of the registered owner and the number of shares owned?
3. Are surrendered stock certificates effectively canceled and attached to the issue stub in the stock certificate books?
4. Are adequate records maintained for stock reserved under options, including optionee, option price, and expiration date?
5. Are stockholders' ledgers and open stubs in the stock certificate books balanced periodically to the general ledger by people who are not authorized to sign new certificates and who are not custodians of the stock certificate book?
6. Are unclaimed dividend checks periodically reviewed, entered as liabilities in the accounts, and restored to cash?
7. Are transfer stamps affixed on the acquisition of outstanding stock?

REFERENCES

Committee on Auditing Standards and Procedures of the Florida Institute of CPAs. *The Internal Control Questionnaire*, 1976.
Scott, Richard, Page, John, and Hooper, Paul. *Auditing: A Systems Approach.* Englewood Cliffs, N.J. Prentice-Hall, 1982.

Index

About the Authors

NEIL H. SNYDER is the Ralph A. Beeton professor at the McIntire School of Commerce at the University of Virginia. In addition, he is director of the school's Center for Entrepreneurial Studies and its management area coordinator. From 1982 to 1985 he served as policy advisor for regulatory reform to then Governor Charles Robb of Virginia. In 1984 he co-chaired and in 1986 he chaired the Governor's Conferences on Small Business in Virginia. In 1985 he received the Virginia Chamber of Commerce Small Business Advocacy Award. He is author or co-author of six books in strategic management, more than three dozen business policy cases and forty-five articles on strategic management issues.

O. WHITFIELD BROOME, JR., is a professor and Director of Graduate Studies at the McIntire School of Commerce at the University of Virginia. He is also a CPA. From 1978 to 1984 he was Executive Director of The Institute of Chartered Financial Analysts, and from 1986 to 1987 he chaired the National CPA Examination Review Board. He has lectured in numerous professional development programs for accountants, bankers and financial analysts. He is a member of the American Institute of Certified Public Accountants, the American Accounting Association, The Financial Analysts Federation, and the Financial Management Association.

WILLIAM J. KEHOE is the Consumer Bankers Association professor and associate dean at the McIntire School of Commerce at the University of Virginia. He is a member of the Society for Business Ethics and was named a research associate for the Center for the Study of Applied Ethics. He is the author or co-author of three books and numerous articles on marketing and ethics issues.

JAMES T. McINTYRE, JR., is an attorney with McNair and Associates in Washington, D.C. He served for three years as director of the Office of Management and Budget and as a member of President Jimmy Carter's Cabinet. In addition to his law practice, he teaches graduate courses in public finance. In 1987 he was appointed by President Ronald Reagan to the President's Commission on Privatization.

KAREN E. BLAIR is a 1987 graduate of the University of Virginia and of the McIntyre Business Institute at the university. She is currently a law student at the University of South Carolina School of Law.